Numbers are keyed to captions throughout the book.

Numbers are keyed to captions throughout the book.

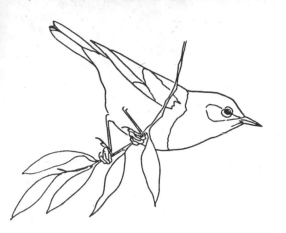

A Field Guide to the Birds Coloring Book

Roger Tory Peterson
and Peter Alden

Illustrations by John Sill

Houghton Mifflin Company   Boston

TOPOGRAPHY OF A BIRD

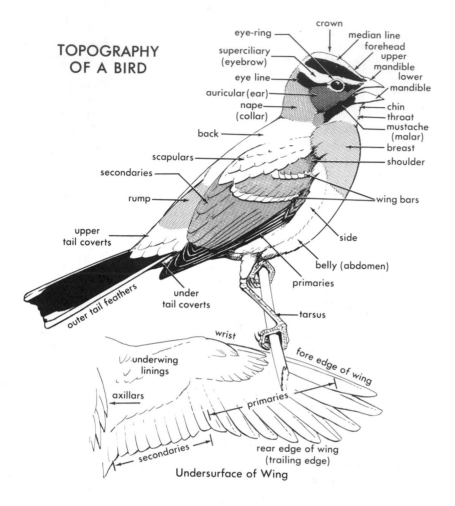

crown
eye-ring
median line
superciliary (eyebrow)
forehead
upper mandible
lower mandible
eye line
auricular (ear)
nape (collar)
chin
throat
mustache (malar)
back
breast
scapulars
shoulder
secondaries
rump
wing bars
upper tail coverts
side
belly (abdomen)
outer tail feathers
under tail coverts
primaries
tarsus
wrist
underwing linings
fore edge of wing
axillars
primaries
secondaries
rear edge of wing (trailing edge)

Undersurface of Wing

Library of Congress Cataloging in Publication Data

Peterson, Roger Tory, date
  A field guide to the birds coloring book.

  1. Birds — North America — Identification. 2. Painting books. I. Alden, Peter. II. Sill, John. III. Title.
QL681.P454 1982   598.297
82-11804
ISBN 0-395-32521-8 (pbk.)

Printed in the United States of America

M 10 9 8 7

Front Cover: Barn Swallow

Introduction

Birdwatching, or "birding," is a visual activity, a game or sport that trains the eye. Most beginning birders soon acquire a copy of *A Field Guide to the Birds* or its western counterpart, *A Field Guide to Western Birds* — handy, pocket-sized books that offer shortcuts to knowing the birds. The birds shown in these Field Guides are reduced to basic shapes and patterns, with arrows pointing to the special field marks by which one kind of bird can be told apart from another.

Although even a person who is colorblind can become skilled at identifying birds by their patterns, color is the best key to most species. This coloring book will sharpen your observations and condition your memory for the days you spend out-of-doors. You will become aware that the reddish color on the underparts of a robin or a bluebird does not extend completely from beak to tail, and that there are small areas of white as well. By filling in the colors during evenings at home or on winter days before the migrants arrive (if you live in the North), you will be better informed about the appearance of these same birds when you see them in life. Binoculars are a big help if you have a pair; a seven- or eight-power glass makes a bird seven or eight times as handsome, but it is not entirely necessary if your eyes are sharp.

A coloring book such as this will help your color perception, but it will not teach you to draw, unless you copy the basic line drawings so artfully prepared by John Sill. You might even try to sketch living birds in the field, if only roughly in pencil.

Watching birds can be many things — an art, a science, a game, or a sport — but above all it is an absorbing activity that sharpens the senses, especially the eye and the ear. If you draw or paint, the sense of touch also comes into play; the images of the eye and the mind are transferred by hand to paper. In the process, you become more aware of the natural world — the real world — and the everyday human world as well.

Most of you may find colored pencils best suited for coloring this book, but if you are handy with brushes and paints, you may prefer to fill in the outlines with watercolors. Crayons, too, can be used. But don't labor; have fun. That is what birding and this coloring book are all about.

Roger Tory Peterson

About This Book

Millions of people have been introduced to birdwatching by Roger Tory Peterson's *A Field Guide to the Birds* and *A Field Guide to Western Birds*. The idea behind this coloring book is to make bird identification even easier, by taking the classic Peterson Field Guide approach one step further. In Field Guides, arrows point to stripes, bars, patches of color, and other distinctive features (called *field marks*) that help you identify each bird you see. Depending on where you live, you may be able to see over a hundred birds a year, without even leaving your neighborhood. Remembering the shapes and color patterns for all those birds is quite a challenge. One of the easiest and most enjoyable ways of learning birds is by drawing them or coloring pictures of them. Once you have colored in the golden slippers of a Snowy Egret, for example, you will be unlikely to forget them. Although there are other clues to a bird's identification — such as the way it moves, its voice, and the kind of place where it lives — its color pattern is a very important key. After you have colored the birds in this book, we think you will find that you have learned how to recognize them in the field.

As a child I spent many enjoyable hours wandering the woods and fields of Concord, Massachusetts. Following in the footsteps of Henry David Thoreau, I discovered many of the plants and animals he had marveled at a century before, and, like him, I was particularly fascinated by the diverse birdlife I saw. In those early years, I took great delight in coloring the bird outlines shown in Audubon Society bird leaflets. I found that it was much easier to learn the color patterns by coloring birds myself, rather than just studying pictures. Today, as I lead groups of birdwatchers on tours to jungles and deserts on six continents, I continue to draw on the enthusiasm and knowledge I gained by coloring birds so many years before. Whether you are a beginner or an experienced birder, I hope that you will find this coloring book to be an enjoyable way to learn more about birds.

How to Use This Book

Birds Included. The birds in this coloring book are the ones we think you are most likely to see. Keep in mind that some birds, such as the Mourning Dove, are found all over North America, while others are common in the East but not the West, or live in the North but not the South, or vice versa. Also, remember that in some kinds of birds both sexes look alike; in others the male is more colorful than the female. For those birds, we usually show just the male (in his colorful breeding plumage), since he is easier to recognize — and more fun to color. Because of the space available, the rarer birds and some females and immatures could not be included in this coloring book, but you can find descriptions and illustrations of them (along with more details about the birds that are shown here) in *A Field Guide to the Birds* and *A Field Guide to Western Birds*.

Species. There are about 9,000 species (or kinds) of birds in the world. Over 600 species of birds regularly occur in North America north of Mexico, and almost half of these are shown in this book. The simplest definition of a species is that the birds in one species will not normally breed with birds of another species. Certain species include different *races*, which may look different but can breed with each other. For example, the Northern Oriole includes two races, the Baltimore Oriole and Bullock's Oriole. The Baltimore and Bullock's look very different and were once thought to be two separate species, but now we know they are just different races of a single species. You may know this bird and others in this book by a slightly different name, but the names we give here are the ones that are most widely accepted across North America.

Families. The birds in this book are arranged according to families. Most families consist of several species. The families appear roughly in the order in which they evolved — from the earliest, most primitive families to the ones that evolved most recently. This is the same order you will find in most checklists for birdwatchers.

Here is an easy way to remember the order: Ocean, shore, game, and predatory birds appear first; these are generally the largest birds. Next are the hole-nesting birds (such as woodpeckers) without true songs; they are generally smaller. Last come the songbirds (the most recently evolved birds), which are smaller still. There are exceptions, of course, but the order of birds in this book progresses roughly from large to medium to small; it also proceeds from birds that eat fish and small mammals to those that eat seeds and insects.

Identifying Birds. As you color the birds in a family, notice the features they have in common. The shape of a bird's bill, for example, can be very useful as a quick way of telling what family the bird belongs to. Waterfowl (swans, ducks, and geese) can be easily recognized by their distinctive bills, and warblers can be told from sparrows by their bills. Although warblers and sparrows (which belong to the finch family) are both small, warblers have needlelike bills, while sparrows have thick, short ones for cracking seeds. Within the larger families of birds, such as hawks, finches, and flycatchers, you should also try to learn the subgroups (genera) of similar species. Then, after studying the distinctive features (field marks) of each bird, try to name the species. Although there are hundreds of species of birds in North

America, these are grouped into only about 80 families. If you can get the family right first, that will narrow down the number of species considerably, making identification much easier. So remember — family first, species second.

Parts of a Bird. In general, we have avoided using technical terms for the parts of a bird in this book. For example, if something looks like an "eyebrow," that's what we call it — not a *superciliary* (the word used by ornithologists — bird scientists). However, if you have only recently become interested in birds, then you will be unfamiliar with some of the terms used to describe them. Study the labeled illustration at the front of this coloring book, which gives the names of the different parts. Most of the basic parts are described below.

Head. Almost every bird can be identified by a view of just the head and the bill, although this takes some practice. Many birds have distinctive stripes or colored patches on the head, which are excellent field marks to use for identifying species. The top of the head is called the *crown*, and if a certain color is present only on the top part of the crown, that area is called the *cap* (as in the Black-capped Chickadee). The area between the eye and the bill is called the *lores*. Some birds have distinctive eyestripes or eye-rings (which are sometimes referred to as "spectacles"). As you color the *eye* of a bird, notice its size. Is it relatively large or small? If the eye is large, the bird probably feeds at night or lives in the shade. Birds do not have visible *ears*. However, some birds, such as certain owls, have tufts that are incorrectly called ears. The area immediately below the bill is called the *chin*. The *throat* is the area between the bill and the breast.

Bill. All birds have a two-part bill consisting of an *upper* and a *lower mandible*. The term beak is sometimes used for the hooked bill of a hawk or parrot. Besides being a good clue to the family a bird belongs to, the shape of the bill will also tell you a great deal about the kinds of food each bird specializes in eating. For example, seed-eaters, such as finches, have thick short bills for cracking seeds; hawks have strong, hooked beaks for tearing flesh; herons have long spearlike bills for catching fish; and flycatchers have wide beaks that are good for snapping up insects.

Body: The upper surface of the body is called the *back*, and the area closer to the tail is the *rump*. Some birds, such as cranes, have very long necks, while most birds show no real *neck* at all. On the underparts, the upper half (closer to the head) is called the *breast* (or *chest*), while the lower half (around the legs) is termed the *belly*. A number of birds have distinctive patterns on their *sides* — the part of the belly just under the wing. Some people confuse *stripes* and *bars*. Remember that stripes run lengthwise (along the

bird's body, from head to tail) while bars run crosswise (from wing to wing).

Tail: Birds use their tails for steering and braking in flight. Some birds also display their tails during courtship. The shape, color patterns, and use of the tail are great aids in identifying species. For example, for some unknown reason, many birds that live near water often wag or bob their tails. As you color the tail, notice its shape. If the outer tail feathers are much longer than the rest, we say that the tail is *forked*, while if they are only slightly longer we say that it is *notched*. In some birds, such as the Ring-necked Pheasant, the central tail feathers are *elongated*.

Legs: As you color the legs of different species of birds, you will notice that they vary in length and thickness — an important clue to the way the bird lives. Swifts and hummingbirds, for example, have very tiny legs and feet that are useful only for clinging; they cannot be used for walking. The kind of feet a bird has can tell you whether it spends most of its time perching, walking, or swimming. Note the wide variety in shapes and adaptations, such as the webbed feet (for swimming) of ducks and gulls, the powerful clawed feet (for catching and holding prey) of eagles, and the feathered feet (for warmth) of grouse.

Wings: Most birds have wings that can be used for true flight, not just gliding. Some birds also use their wings for balance, whether they are soaring in strong winds, hovering in relatively still air, or perching on a branch or fencepost. Wings may also be displayed as part of courtship. As you color a bird's wings, notice whether they are particularly long or short, pointed or rounded. Many birds have prominent black, white or colored patches on the wing, which are useful in identification. The leading edge of the wing (nearest the body) is often called the *shoulder*. Behind the forward half of the wing (where the bones and muscles are located) are two sets of flight feathers. The ones closer to the body — from the bend of the wing inward — are known as *secondaries*. The flight feathers from the bend of the wing to the tip are the *primaries*.

A Final Word. There are millions of birdwatchers in North America. Although millions of them belong to Audubon societies and other nature groups, much birdwatching is done alone or in small groups. When you first go out on your own to watch birds, you will find quite a number of them that will be hard to identify. We hope that this coloring book will make it easier for you to identify birds, by making you a better observer. Keep track of all the birds you see (including when and where you saw them) in notebooks, and sketch and color any birds that you cannot identify. Birdwatching is one of the most worthwhile mental and physical pastimes. Enjoy yourself and keep learning.

Peter Alden

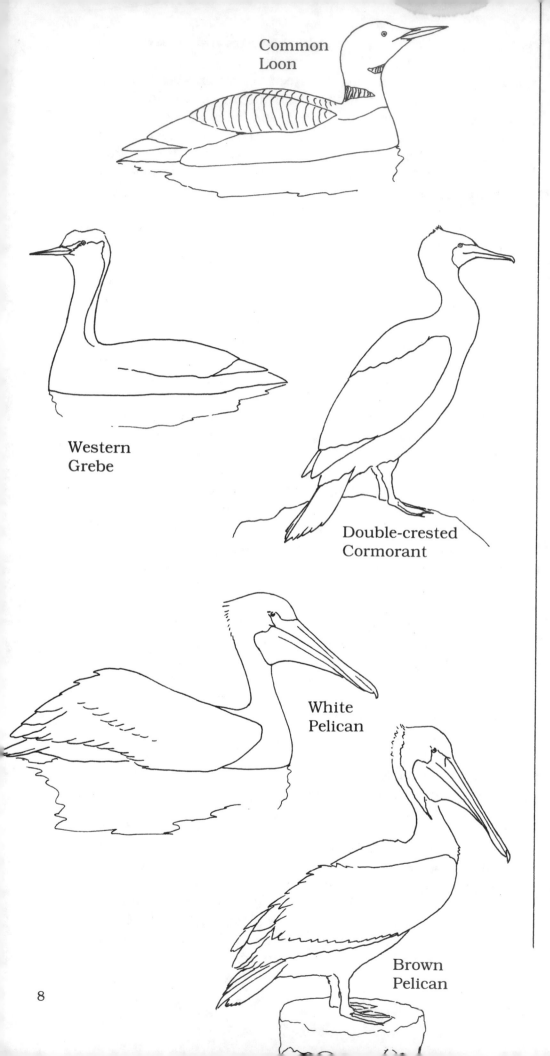

Common Loon A huge duck-like bird that dives for fish from the surface of forest-fringed northern lakes. On summer nights, its yodels jar the night air and sound almost human. In breeding plumage (shown), the loon has a dark greenish black head and a black and white checkered back. In winter it becomes gray above and white below, and is found on the ocean or on bays. (1)

Western Grebe A black and white, long-necked swimmer of western lakes, marshes, and (in winter) coastal waters. The bill is yellow and the eye is red. Like other grebes, this bird carries its young on its back. (2)

Pied-billed Grebe (in Pond Scene, p. 15) (3)

Double-crested Cormorant A blackish fish-eater, also known as the "shag" or "sea crow." It nests in trees on inland lakes and on rocky islands in the ocean. The head, neck, and underparts are an oily dark green; the face and small throat pouch are orange. Notice the slight hook at the end of this bird's bill. (4)

White Pelican One of our largest birds, with a wingspread of 9 ft. It breeds near western lakes and winters on our southern coasts. A group of White Pelicans can form a semicircle around a school of fish and drive the fish toward shallow water, where they can be scooped up from the surface. The bill and legs of this bird are orange-yellow; the flight feathers are black. (5)

Brown Pelican A view of this great bird diving headfirst into the warm waters off our southern coasts evokes images of pterodactyls. In breeding plumage, the head of this bird is yellow and the neck is a rich chestnut color. (6)

Herons, Egrets, and Bitterns

Long-legged, long-necked wading birds that feed chiefly on fish, which they spear with their long bills in shallow waters. These birds should not be confused with cranes (p. 23), which are primarily vegetarians. Herons often nest in large colonies on trees near swamps and fly many miles to their feeding grounds every day. In flight, the head and neck are folded into a giant S.

Great Blue Heron Our largest and most widespread heron (sometimes mistakenly called the "Blue Crane"). The yellow bill and chestnut-colored thighs contrast with the pastel blue and gray feathers on the body. (7)

Great Egret The largest of our white herons, with a very long neck, a long yellow bill, and black legs. Like the Snowy Egret, this bird was once endangered by plume hunters, but was rescued by the Audubon movement. (8)

Little Blue Heron This bird comes in two color phases: a *dark phase*, which is blue-gray with a reddish purple head and neck; and a *white phase*, which looks like the white plumage of an egret. (In egrets, however, the bill is all black or all yellow, not grayish with a black tip.) Immature Little Blue Herons are also white. (9)

Snowy Egret Another beautiful bird that was hunted for its plumes but was saved by the Audubon movement. In breeding season, it develops gorgeous long plumes on the head, neck, and back. This elegant bird is white, with a slender black bill, long black legs, and contrasting yellow feet ("golden slippers"). (10)

Great Blue Heron

Great Egret

adult, dark phase

Little Blue Heron

immature

Snowy Egret

9

Louisiana
Heron

*non-breeding
plumage*

breeding plumage

Cattle
Egret

Black-crowned
Night Heron

adult

immature

Yellow-crowned
Night Heron

Louisiana Heron A slender dark heron with a white belly and a white rump. The head, neck, and body are various shades of slate-gray, purple, brown, and other colors in both adults and immatures (birds that are too young to breed), but the belly is always white. (11)

Cattle Egret Not a true fishing egret. This African bird has recently colonized North and South America (without the help of man), and is often found in fields near cattle. It has a yellow beak like the Great Egret, but is a much smaller bird. All-white most of the year, it develops buffy plumes in summer. (12)

Black-crowned Night Heron Note the extra-large eyes that this heron and most other nocturnal birds have. In adults, the eye is red, the back dark green. Immatures are brown with white spots. Also active during the day — often seen flying overhead at dawn and at dusk, even in cities! (13)

Yellow-crowned Night Heron Another chunky little night heron, found chiefly in saltwater areas of the southeastern U.S. In this species the adults are pearly gray all over, with reddish orange eyes and a black and white face. The crown is more whitish than yellow. (14)

American Bittern (15) (in Marsh Scene, p. 25)

Green Heron (16) (in Marsh Scene, p. 25)

Wood Stork A magnificent wading bird of the swamps in the southeastern U.S. This stork nests in colonies in huge trees. It is white with a bare (unfeathered) gray head and neck and black flight feathers. The down-curved bill is black in adults, yellow in immatures. (17)

Glossy Ibis An eastern ibis, found in colonies in marshes. It is dark rusty overall, with glossy greenish wings and a long, down-curved bill. Sometimes it looks almost black at a distance. Unlike a heron, it flies with its neck extended. (18a) The **White Ibis** lives in southeastern marshes. It has a red face and a drooping bill (see close-up of head). Brilliant red legs and black ("dipped in ink") wingtips accent its snowy white plumage. (18b)

Roseate Spoonbill One of our most colorful birds, found in coastal marshes and lagoons around the Gulf of Mexico. Its grotesque bare head features a long, spoon-shaped bill, which gives the bird its name. It has a pink (roseate) back, bright red shoulders and legs, and an orange tail. (19)

American Flamingo Occasionally seen in Florida, usually as strays from breeding colonies in the West Indies. This pink bird has the longest legs and neck of any North American bird. (20)

Wood Stork

White Ibis

Glossy Ibis

American Flamingo

Roseate Spoonbill

11

Whistling
Swan

Mute
Swan

Canada Goose

Swans

These huge, snowy white waterbirds are a thrill to see. Like dabbling ducks (p. 14), they tip down to feed on underwater plants. However, because of their longer necks, swans can eat food that is beyond the reach of the dabblers. In flight, swans hold their necks straight out, unlike herons or egrets, which fly with their necks pulled into an S.

Whistling Swan Breeds on the Arctic tundra in the summer; migrates south in large V-shaped flocks to lakes and shores in the U.S. for the winter. This huge white swan often has a yellow spot at the base of its smooth black bill. (21)

Mute Swan Introduced from northern Europe; now common on coastal lagoons in the Northeast. This swan can be recognized by the black knob on top of its orange bill. When swimming it holds its neck in a curve, and often folds its wings over its back like a fan. (22)

Geese

These waterfowl are larger than ducks but smaller than swans. In ducks, the males usually are more colorful than the females, but in geese and swans both sexes look alike. Flocks of geese honking overhead as they migrate in V-shaped lines are a sign of the changing seasons.

Canada Goose The symbol of our National Wildlife Refuges. Often seen migrating in V-formations in fall or spring; becoming a year-round resident in an increasing number of areas. The fluffy yellow goslings grow up into huge brown geese with long black necks and black heads, sporting a distinctive white chinstrap. (23)

Brant A miniature look-alike of the Canada Goose, with a partial white necklace instead of a white chinstrap. It spends the winter on our coasts, where it feeds on eelgrass. (24)

White-fronted Goose Common in winter in the South and West. The adults are pink-billed, with a distinct white face patch, strong black bars on the belly, and yellow legs. (25)

Snow Goose Breeds in the high Arctic and winters in coastal fields and marshes farther south. Two color phases: a *white phase*, with a pink bill and legs, and black wing tips (26); and a *dark phase* (called the "Blue Goose"), which is more common in the East. The Blue Goose is slate-gray, with paler bluish wings. Only its head, neck, and belly are white.

Dabbling (Tipping) Ducks

Unlike diving ducks, sea ducks, and mergansers (p. 16), these ducks rarely dive for food. Instead, they dabble on the surface, tipping their heads and stretching their necks down to feed in shallow water. The tips of their tails stick up in the air while they nibble on plants underwater.

Mallard (27) (in Pond Scene, p. 15)

American Black Duck An eastern duck, closely related to the Mallard. Both sexes are much darker brown than the female Mallard. In flight, the Black Duck looks blackish with brilliant white underwing linings. (28)

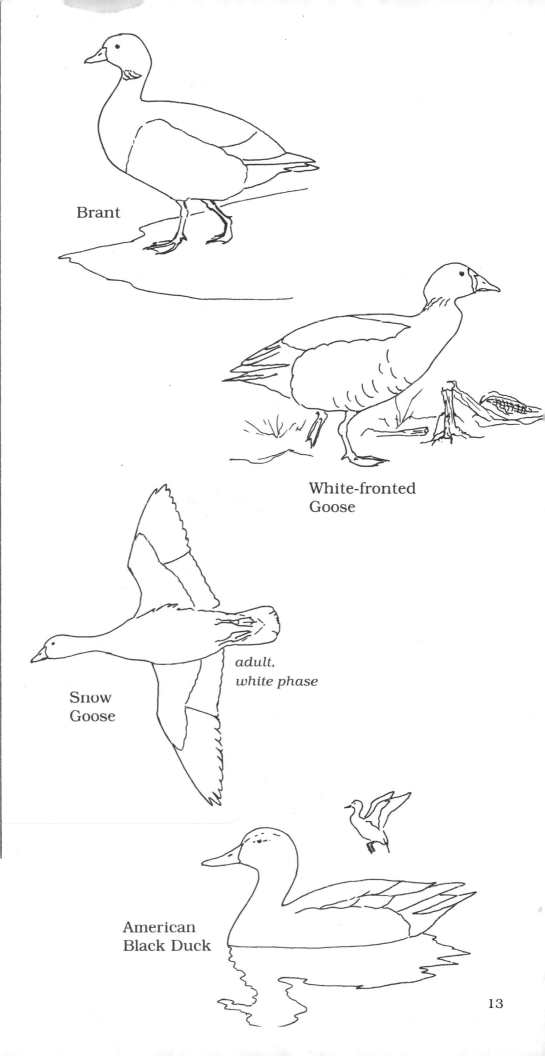

Brant

White-fronted Goose

Snow Goose

adult, white phase

American Black Duck

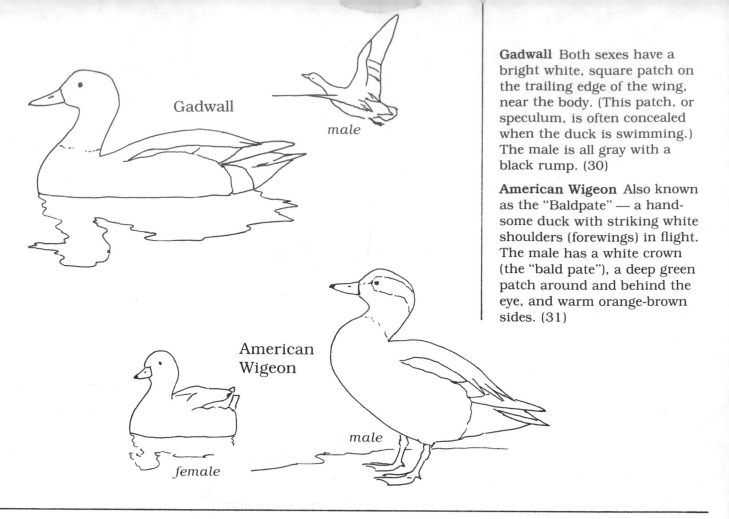

Gadwall

male

American Wigeon

female

male

Gadwall Both sexes have a bright white, square patch on the trailing edge of the wing, near the body. (This patch, or speculum, is often concealed when the duck is swimming.) The male is all gray with a black rump. (30)

American Wigeon Also known as the "Baldpate" — a handsome duck with striking white shoulders (forewings) in flight. The male has a white crown (the "bald pate"), a deep green patch around and behind the eye, and warm orange-brown sides. (31)

Pond Scene

If you visit a pond, lake, or reservoir at the right time of year, you are likely to find a variety of waterfowl there. Notice the amazing variations in color patterns on the ducks (especially the males). Many of these birds become quite tame on ponds where no hunting is ever allowed, or in areas where people feed them during the cooler months. Except for the grebe, all these birds are dabbling ducks.

Pied-billed Grebe The most widespread grebe in North America. This bird dives for fish in quiet ponds and lakes. It is dusky brown all over, and has a conspicuous black ring on its thick silver bill. This *pied* bill gives the bird its name. (3)

Mallard The world's most widespread duck. The male, or *drake*, is resplendent with his glossy green head, yellow bill, white necklace, chestnut chest, and black feathers curled-up over the white tail. The female is buffy and mottled with darker brown. Both sexes have a shiny bluish patch on the wing, called the *speculum*. (27)

Common Pintail Our most streamlined duck, with a long neck and an elongated tail (which is even longer in the male). In the male, the head is a rich dark brown, the neck and breast are white, the sides and back are gray, and the long thin tail is mostly black. (29)

Wood Duck One of the most beautiful ducks in the world — a virtual rainbow on wings. This duck lives in wooded swamps and nests in tree hollows or in nesting boxes set out in marshes specifically for Wood Ducks. (32)

Northern Shoveler A dabbler with a short neck and a very long shovel-like bill. The male's head is green (as in the Mallard) but his bill is black, his eye is yellow, his chest is white, and his sides are chestnut-colored. (33)

Green-winged Teal One of North America's smallest ducks. A fast flier, found from coast to coast. The drake (shown) has a handsome chestnut head with a green patch around and behind the eye. Both sexes have only a small patch of green on the wings, on the secondaries. This distinctive green patch is hard to see when the teal is on the water, but is more noticeable in flight. (34)

14

Pond Scene

15

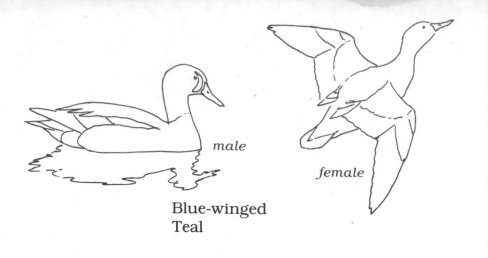

Blue-winged
Teal

Cinnamon
Teal

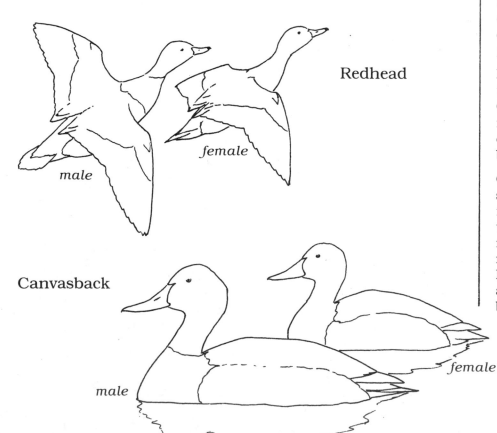

Redhead

Canvasback

Blue-winged Teal Looks like a small shoveler. Both ducks have powder-blue shoulders (forewings), which are more visible in flight. The male Blue-wing is a warm buff color, with dark streaks on the back and spots on the belly. He also has a strong white crescent on his face. (35)

Cinnamon Teal A western teal that resembles the Blue-wing in flight. Both teals are about the same size and shape, with the same powder-blue shoulders, but the male Cinnamon Teal has a dark chestnut head and body. (36)

Diving Ducks and Sea Ducks

These ducks all dive deep into lakes, rivers, and oceans for their food. Most are fast fliers. The ducks below breed in the Arctic or on midwestern prairies, and are seen by people near the coast only in the winter months. The first six are diving ducks, which are found on lakes and in estuaries. The others are mostly sea ducks that are found on coastal bays and rivers and on the open ocean during much of the year.

Redhead A diving duck with a typical duck's bill, unlike the Canvasback. The male has a reddish chestnut head, a black chest, and a uniformly gray body. (37)

Canvasback Note the long swanlike bill and the low sloping forehead. Except for this, the male looks much like a male Redhead, with the chestnut head and the black chest. However, the male Canvasback also is much lighter on the back (whitish, not gray). (38)

Ring-necked Duck Another diving duck with a black chest. The male has a bit of a tuft on the head, and a reddish neckring that is not very conspicuous. His head is purple and his back is black, contrasting with the gray-white feathers below. Both sexes have a white ring and a dark tip on the bill. (39)

Lesser Scaup Common in winter on coastal bays, estuaries, and lakes. The male is very similar to a male Ring-neck with a purple head, yellow eye, and black chest, but his back is gray, not black. (40)
The **Greater Scaup** (not shown) is slightly larger, with a green head and whiter sides (in the male).

Common Goldeneye A striking diving duck that breeds near northern lakes and winters on cold oceans, rivers, and inlets. The male has a green head with a bright yellow eye and a large, round white spot on the "cheek." His body is black above, white below. (41)

Bufflehead A cute little diving duck that spends its winters on our lowland waters (bays and estuaries). The male is mostly white with a black back and glossy black head, accented by a large white patch. (42)

White-winged Scoter A blackish sea duck with a swollen bill. The white patch on the trailing edge of the wing is hard to see until the bird flaps or takes off. The male also has a white "teardrop" below the eye. (43a)
The **Surf Scoter** is similar but the male has two white patches on the crown and the nape. (see close-up of head, 43b). This scoter is often seen in rough seas just beyond the surf, on both our coasts.

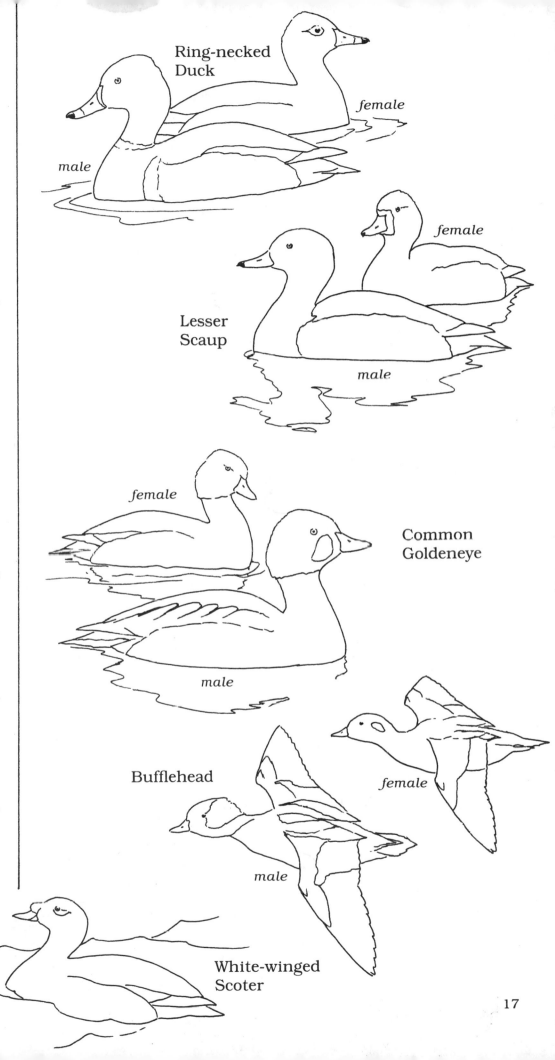

Ring-necked Duck

female

male

Lesser Scaup

female

male

female

Common Goldeneye

male

Bufflehead

female

male

White-winged Scoter

Surf Scoter

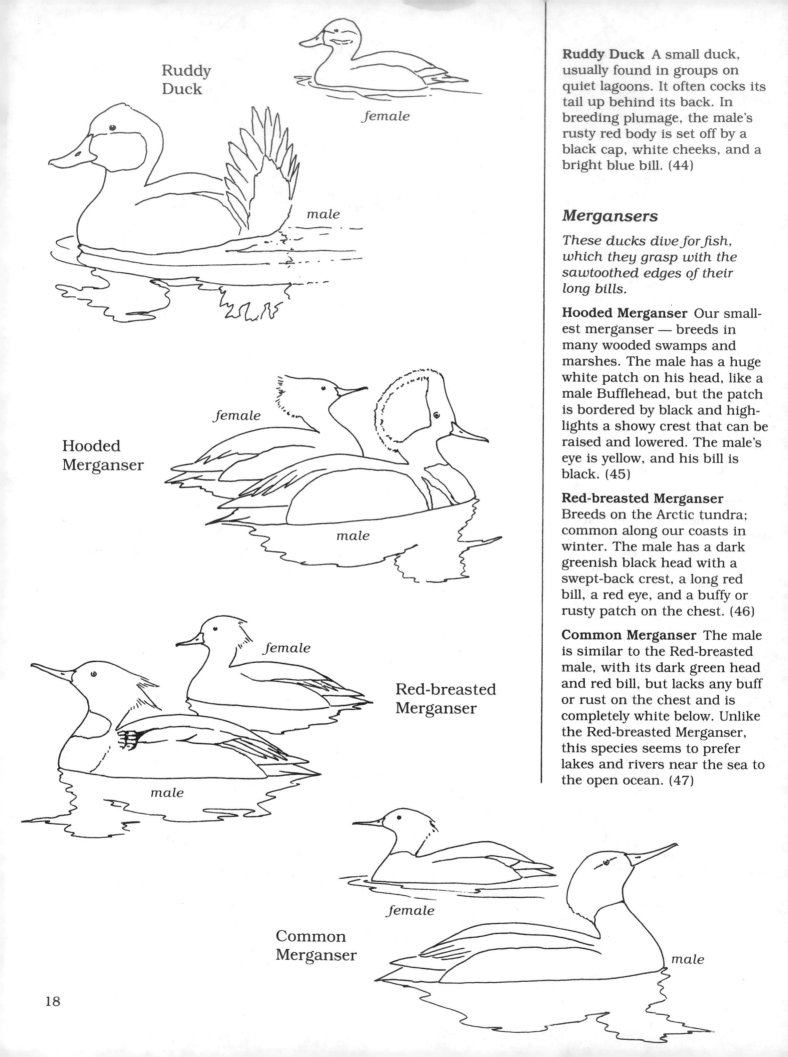

Ruddy
Duck

female

male

Hooded
Merganser

female

male

female

Red-breasted
Merganser

male

Common
Merganser

female

male

Ruddy Duck A small duck, usually found in groups on quiet lagoons. It often cocks its tail up behind its back. In breeding plumage, the male's rusty red body is set off by a black cap, white cheeks, and a bright blue bill. (44)

Mergansers

These ducks dive for fish, which they grasp with the sawtoothed edges of their long bills.

Hooded Merganser Our smallest merganser — breeds in many wooded swamps and marshes. The male has a huge white patch on his head, like a male Bufflehead, but the patch is bordered by black and highlights a showy crest that can be raised and lowered. The male's eye is yellow, and his bill is black. (45)

Red-breasted Merganser Breeds on the Arctic tundra; common along our coasts in winter. The male has a dark greenish black head with a swept-back crest, a long red bill, a red eye, and a buffy or rusty patch on the chest. (46)

Common Merganser The male is similar to the Red-breasted male, with its dark green head and red bill, but lacks any buff or rust on the chest and is completely white below. Unlike the Red-breasted Merganser, this species seems to prefer lakes and rivers near the sea to the open ocean. (47)

Vultures

The true vultures of the New World are blackish, with naked (unfeathered) heads and weak feet. They soar for long periods looking for dead and dying animals. "Buzzard" is a name for true hawks in the Old World, and should not be used for vultures.

Turkey Vulture Our most widespread vulture, which is expanding its range in the Northeast. It glides rather than flaps and is found soaring over forests, plains, and mountains. It has a bare red head and long upswept wings with paler silver flight feathers that make the wings look two-toned. (48)

Black Vulture A short-tailed vulture that typically flaps three times, soars, and flaps three more times. This vulture is more common in the Southeast. (49)

Swallow-tailed Kite A spectacular aerial acrobat that soars over wooded swamps in the South, looking for snakes in the treetops. This striking bird is snowy white, with a long black forked tail and black flight feathers. (50)

Osprey A huge bird of prey, with a wingspread of about 6 feet. It is dark brown above, with a white crest and underparts. This "fish hawk" spots fish while flying over rivers, lakes, and estuaries, then swoops down to catch them with its powerful feet. (51)

Sharp-shinned Hawk A small bird hawk (accipiter) that flies through woodlands pursuing small birds, such as warblers and sparrows. It is slate gray above, with rusty bars on the breast. The short rounded wings and long, narrow, square-cut tail are marked with dark bars. (52)

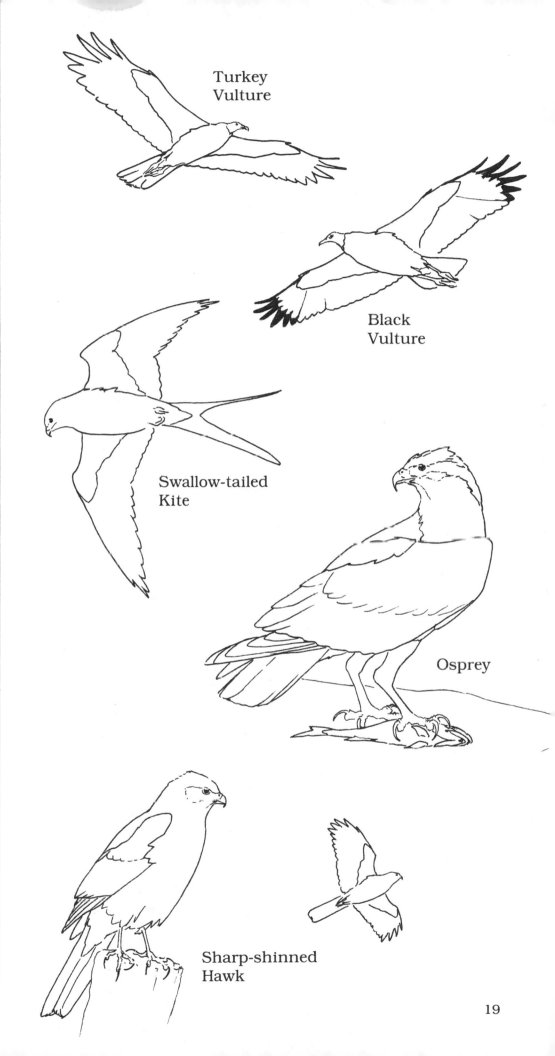

Turkey Vulture

Black Vulture

Swallow-tailed Kite

Osprey

Sharp-shinned Hawk

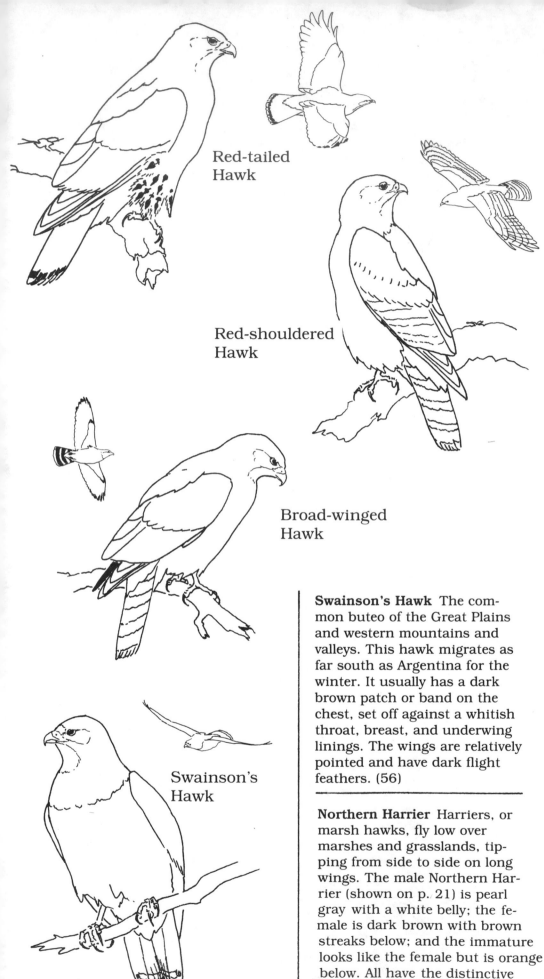

Red-tailed Hawk

Red-shouldered Hawk

Broad-winged Hawk

Swainson's Hawk

Buteos

These are the large hawks with fan-shaped tails that are often seen soaring on their long broad wings or sitting in a dead tree by a highway. Mistakenly called "chicken hawks," buteos are actually helpful in controlling rodent populations.

Red-tailed Hawk The most common and widespread large hawk in North America. The tail is rusty orange in all adults, but the coloring of the rest of the body varies widely. Typical birds have a white chest, with contrasting dark streaks on the neck and the belly. Other Red-tails can be blackish, reddish, or white below, with few streaks. This hawk feeds chiefly on small mammals. (53)

Red-shouldered Hawk A beautiful hawk, usually found in wetter woodlands and swamps, where it feeds on frogs, snakes, and other small animals. The shoulders are rusty and the tail has broad dark bands on both sides. The breast and underwing linings are rusty, with heavy orange bars; the flight feathers have prominent black and white bars. (54)

Broad-winged Hawk The most common hawk of the eastern forests in summer. In April and September it migrates in great numbers along the ridges of the Appalachians. The wings are slate gray above, whitish below. The tail is evenly banded with black and white (above and below) and the breast and belly are whitish with rusty bars. (55)

Eagles

The name "eagle" is applied to several groups of large hawks, some of which are not very closely related. In North America we have two magnificent eagles — the Golden and the

Swainson's Hawk The common buteo of the Great Plains and western mountains and valleys. This hawk migrates as far south as Argentina for the winter. It usually has a dark brown patch or band on the chest, set off against a whitish throat, breast, and underwing linings. The wings are relatively pointed and have dark flight feathers. (56)

Northern Harrier Harriers, or marsh hawks, fly low over marshes and grasslands, tipping from side to side on long wings. The male Northern Harrier (shown on p. 21) is pearl gray with a white belly; the female is dark brown with brown streaks below; and the immature looks like the female but is orange below. All have the distinctive white rump. (57)

Bald. The powerful flight of these huge birds is an unforgettable sight.

Golden Eagle A powerful eagle of western mountains and plains, which is making a comeback in the remote wooded hills of the Northeast. The adult is brown with a gold nape; the immature is similar but has a white stripe under its wings and a white patch at the base of its tail. This eagle feeds on many rodents (such as ground squirrels) that damage crops and pastures. (58)

Bald Eagle Our national bird — easily recognized by its white head and tail, dark brown body, and yellow legs and beak. (The head and most of the tail are dark in immature birds.) Some people think this bird should have been named the American Sea-Eagle because it is more like a fishing vulture in its feeding habits. (59)

Falcons

These fast-flying birds of prey have medium-long, very pointed wings.

Peregrine Falcon Perhaps the fastest flying bird in the world. This endangered species is making a comeback, thanks to captive-breeding specialists and laws restricting the use of pesticides. The Peregrine is slaty above, with distinctive black "sideburns" and a rusty or buffy breast, with fine dark streaks or bars. The feet and the cere (which covers the top part of the beak, or upper mandible) are yellow (60a). The **Prairie Falcon** takes the place of the Peregrine on many western plains and mountains. This bird is brownish (not slate gray) above, with less noticeable sideburns (see close-up of head, 60b). A black patch (where the wings meet the body) is visible from below.

Northern Harrier

Golden Eagle

immature

adult

Bald Eagle

Peregrine Falcon

Prairie Falcon

21

American Kestrel

male

female

Ruffed Grouse

female

Ring-necked Pheasant

male

female

Common Bobwhite

male

Wild Turkey

male

female

American Kestrel A hovering falcon that feeds on large insects (and some birds and rodents) in open country; mistakenly called the "Sparrow Hawk" for many years. The adult male is attractive, with his rusty cap, back, and tail, set off against his blue-gray wings and buffy breast. Both sexes have a blue-gray stripe on the head, with dark "sideburns" below it. (61)

Ruffed Grouse A bird of the deep woods in the North and East. In spring, the males beat the air with their wings, producing a drumming sound. Warm brown all over, except for a black neck patch; the tail can be reddish or grayish and has a dark band at the tip. (62)

Ring-necked Pheasant A magnificent gamebird, originally introduced into the U.S. from China. The male is a rainbow of iridescent colors, especially on the head, which is greenish with a patch of bare red skin around the eye. (Some males lack the white neck-ring.) The female is warm brown with dark mottling. (63)

Common Bobwhite Found in coveys near farmlands in the East and South. The distinctive call of this quail does sound like *bob-white*. Both sexes are reddish brown, but the male sports a white eyebrow and throat patch. (64)

Wild Turkey The bird that would have been our national symbol, if Ben Franklin had had his way. This ancestor of the domestic turkey is now regaining some of its lost habitat in the Northeast; it is still common in parts of the South and Southwest. The male is dark bronze, with a "beard" on his chest; his bare (unfeathered) head is bluish on top, with red wattles on the front of the neck. (65)

Cranes

These big long-legged birds superficially resemble herons, but herons are fish-eaters and cranes are mainly vegetarians (that eat mostly roots, berries, and waste grains). Cranes also have shorter bills (for their size) and fly with their necks outstretched. They have musical calls.

Sandhill Crane This crane is still common from Texas to the prairies of Canada; local elsewhere. It is uniformly soft gray, with a red patch of bare skin on the crown, black legs and bill, and a short, fluffy gray tail. (66)

Whooping Crane Formerly widespread; now an endangered species that winters on the Gulf Coast of Texas and breeds in northeastern Alberta. It is larger than the Sandhill, and is all white except for the black wingtips and the red face and crown. The bill is yellow at the base and the legs are black. (67)

Rails, Gallinules, and Coots

This family includes a variety of birds, all found in swamps and marshes, where they feed on seeds of aquatic plants and insects. Except for the coot, most of these birds are rarely seen. You are more likely to hear their exciting, penetrating calls.

Virginia Rail (68) (in Marsh Scene, p. 25)

Limpkin A long-legged wading bird that looks like a heron or an ibis but is more like a giant rail that feeds on snails. Its haunting calls echo only from the swamps and marshes of the southeastern U.S. It is brown with whitish spots on the neck and a long, curved bill. (69)

Purple Gallinule (70) (in Marsh Scene, p. 25)

American Coot A rail that swims around like a duck, tipping and diving from the surface of freshwater ponds and estuaries (where fresh and salt water meet). It is a powdery slate blue all over, with a thick white bill and a red eye. Also known as the "Mudhen." (71)

Sandhill Crane

immature

adult

Whooping Crane

immature

adult

Limpkin

American Coot

23

Black-necked Stilt

American Avocet

American Oystercatcher

Black-necked Stilt Found on mudflats and in shallow bays in the Southeast; also in marshes and shallow lakes in the West. The stilt is like a huge sandpiper, with very long red legs and a long, thin, straight black bill. It is black above, white below. (72)

American Avocet Another long-necked bird, usually found with the Stilt. It has long bluish legs, a strongly upturned black bill, and two large white stripes on its black wings and back. The head and neck are rusty in summer, white in winter. (73)

American Oystercatcher Found on beaches and mussel beds from New England to Texas. This oystercatcher has a long, chisel-like orange bill, an orange eye-ring, yellow eyes, and pink legs. The head and neck are black, the back brown, and the belly white. (74)

Marsh Scene

Somewhere nearby, you may have a freshwater marsh with cattails, shallow water, and a host of birds that do not live in woodlands, dry fields, or backyards. Some marsh birds are shy, so you must be quiet and make your visits just after dawn or just before dusk. Visit the marsh throughout the year and keep track of the different birds that migrate through there as the seasons progress.

American Bittern A solitary, elusive heron, found only in marshes. Often sticks its bill straight up when discovered. With the buffy streaks on its breast, this bird looks a bit like an immature night heron, but it is a warmer brown and has a black stripe on the neck. (15)

Green Heron A small dark heron, often found alone along wooded streams. Also called the "Little Heron." Although the wings are dark green, much of the head, neck, and breast are a ruddy chestnut color. The legs, which are relatively short for a heron, are bright orange. (16)

Virginia Rail A secretive bird that is actually quite common in most cattail swamps. It is smaller than other rails but has the typical long, down-curved bill. This rail has gray cheeks, chestnut wings, a warm buffy breast, and black and white bars on the belly. In addition to grunts and squeals it utters a loud *kid-ick, kid-ick.* (68)

Purple Gallinule One of North America's most beautiful birds, found in swamps and marshes in the southeastern U.S. It is dark purple, with a green back and wings, a white crown, and bright yellow legs. Its bill is red with a yellow tip. (70)

Spotted Sandpiper One of the few sandpipers that breeds in the U.S.; found teetering up and down near streams as well as on lakeshores. In summer it has heavy black spots like a Wood Thrush (see p. 27) and an orange area at the base of its bill (84). It has a white eyebrow all year round.

Common Snipe A bird that makes noise (a pulsating hum) with its wing feathers during courtship flights. At first glance, this bird looks like the Woodcock, but its neck and legs are longer. It also prefers open marshes, not woodland thickets. The Snipe has a finely striped dark brown back; it is a light buffy color below. (87)

Marsh Scene

15

16

70

68

87

winter   84

25

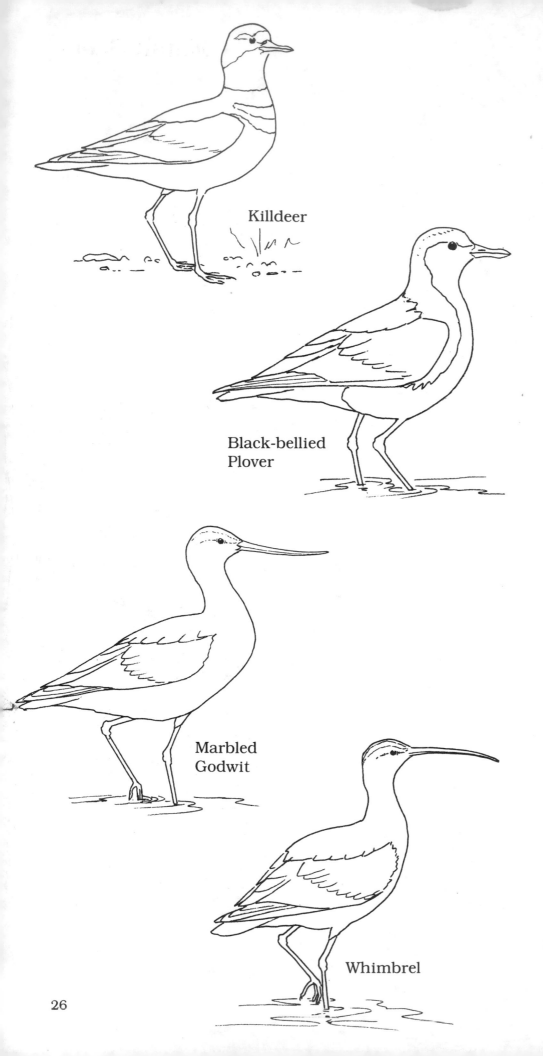

Killdeer

Black-bellied
Plover

Marbled
Godwit

Whimbrel

Plovers

*These birds resemble sand-
pipers (the next family) in several ways: All of them have
short straight bills, medium-
length legs, and pointed
wings. Each kind of plover can
be identified by the distinctive
black and white markings or
stripes on the head and wings.
Plovers run around on mudflats and open grasslands,
pecking for food.*

Killdeer Widespread in open
areas throughout North America. Its *kill-dee* call is often
heard in ball parks, parking
lots, fields, and near lakes.
Unlike most other plovers, it
has two black neck bands, not
just one. (75)

Semipalmated Plover (76) (in
Shore Scene, p. 29)

Black-bellied Plover Our largest plover — breeds in the high
Arctic; quite common on our
shores in spring and fall. In
spring it is spotted gray above,
with white shoulders, a white
rump, and a black belly (as
shown). In the fall it is gray
overall, with dark spots. (77)

Sandpipers

*Most of these are brownish
birds with long legs. Their bills
come in a wide variety of
shapes and sizes. They feed
on exposed shores and open
marshes by probing the mud
and sand with their bills,
searching for insects, worms,
and crustaceans. The sight of
a tightly wheeling flock of
sandpipers on the wing is a
delight to the eye.*

Marbled Godwit A large shore-
bird with long legs and a long,
slightly upturned bill. This bird
is common in the West and
South. It is a warm buff color
with pink at the base of its bill.
(78)

Whimbrel A type of curlew, with a long, down-curved bill; found on prairies and mudflats. It is spotted with dark brown and has conspicuous dark brown head stripes and black legs. (79)

Long-billed Curlew A huge buffy curlew with an extremely long, down-curved bill. It breeds near lakes on prairies and winters on our southern shores. (80)

Upland Sandpiper Breeds in grasslands (prairies and open meadows) in the Great Plains and the Midwest, occasionally even in the East. It is buff or brown overall, with darker mottling and a dark stripe over the eye. The bill is much shorter (for the bird's size) than in the Greater Yellowlegs (see Shore Scene, p. 29). (81)

Greater Yellowlegs (82) (in Shore Scene, p. 29)

Willet A common sandpiper of the West, the South, and (increasingly) the East. This stocky gray bird looks quite plain when feeding on the shore, but is surprisingly attractive in flight, with its striking black and white wings. (83)

Spotted Sandpiper (84) (in Marsh Scene, p. 25)

Ruddy Turnstone (85) (in Shore Scene, p. 29)

American Woodcock The "timberdoodle" — a short-legged bird with a big head, almost no visible neck, and a very long bill. Probes for earthworms and other food in shaded swamps and wet thickets near springs, rather than on open mudflats. During courtship, the male puts on an exciting aerial display. (86)

Common Snipe (87) (in Marsh Scene, p. 25)

Long-billed Curlew

Upland Sandpiper

Willet

Spotted Sandpiper

summer plumage

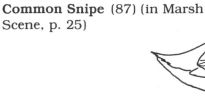

American Woodcock

Short-billed
Dowitcher

Least
Sandpiper

Short-billed Dowitcher Looks like a sewing machine as it bobs up and down, probing for food on the mudflats. Despite its name, this bird has a long straight bill, which makes it look like a Snipe without the stripes on the back. In summer, it is rusty overall, with gray wings and a white rump. (88)

Least Sandpiper Our smallest sandpiper. (The tiny sandpipers are collectively known as "peep.") This bird has yellow-green legs, a rusty wash on its finely spotted breast, and a thin bill. (90)

Shore Scene

There is something special about visiting the coast or backwaters of a tidal slough when the sandpipers and plovers are passing through. Many of these birds wheel in fantastic flight formations, and show a great variety in "personality" in the ways they feed. Some scurry about at a fast pace; others are slower and more methodical in their search for the insects and worms on the mudflats. Shorebirds can be told apart by their distinctive bill and leg shapes, sizes, and colors.

Semipalmated Sandpiper Another "peep," slightly larger and grayer than the Least. This sandpiper also has black legs and a thicker bill. Like the Least, it prefers freshwater marshes and coastal estuaries rather than open sandy beaches. (91)

Dunlin A small sandpiper with a down-curved bill, like a curlew's. This bird is dull gray most of the year, but during breeding season it sports a chestnut back and cap, and has an irregular black patch on its belly, as shown here. (92)

Semipalmated Plover This bird looks like a miniature Killdeer, but with only one breastband. Its back is the color of wet sand. It is usually seen during migration and in winter, in estuaries or along lakeshores. (76)

Greater Yellowlegs A common, fairly large sandpiper with long yellow legs and a slightly upturned bill. The bill is pale gray (and quite thick) at the base, black at the tip. The call of this bird (*kew-kew*) is also distinctive (82). The **Lesser Yellowlegs** (not shown) is similar, but smaller, with a straight bill that is thinner and shorter. Both birds have a white rump, which is visible in flight.

Ruddy Turnstone Usually seen on rocks near the shore or among clumps of seaweed. This bird is quite striking in breeding plumage, with a black and white "harlequin" pattern on its head and breast. The back and wings are a rich chestnut color and the legs are bright orange. (85)

Sanderling A plump sandpiper that seems to be constantly running along the edge of the waves as it feeds on our outer beaches. It is pale gray and white most of the year, but becomes speckled with rusty red in late spring. (89)

82

85

76

89

summer

winter

92

91

Greater
Black-backed
Gull

Herring Gull

California Gull

Ring-billed
Gull

Laughing
Gull

Gulls

These large, long-winged birds have a heavy bill that is as long as the head. Most of them are gray or black on the upper part of the wings and back. Their webbed feet are well-adapted for swimming. The shrill voices of these birds are often heard at refuse dumps as well as near lakes and other waterways — not just at the seashore.

Greater Black-backed Gull A huge gull with black wings and a black back — one of the more common gulls on Atlantic beaches and refuse dumps. It has pink legs and a yellow bill with a red spot (93).

Herring Gull Our most familiar gull — the standard "Jonathan Livingston Seagull." This gull is found around the world and is taking advantage of man's garbage dumps — a ready source of food — to increase its numbers and expand its range. Adult birds (shown) have pink legs and a yellow bill with a red spot. As in most gull species, the immatures (young birds) are brownish. (94)

California Gull A western gull, found on inland marshes and lakes as well as along the Pacific Coast. This bird is famous for saving the Mormons' crops from a locust invasion. It is similar to the Herring Gull, but has yellow-green legs and a black spot on its bill. (95)

Ring-billed Gull Similar to the Herring Gull but smaller, with a complete black ring around the yellow bill. The legs are yellow instead of pink. This gull is found along many inland rivers and lakes as well as at the seashore. (96)

Laughing Gull One of several small-to-medium gulls that develop black heads during the breeding season. This bird is abundant from Cape Cod to Texas. Its bill and legs are a deep red, and its back and wings are a dark slaty color. (97)

Franklin's Gull A "prairie gull" that nests in colonies in freshwater marshes on prairies west of the Great Lakes. This gull follows farmers' tractors and eats worms and grasshoppers that are disturbed during plowing. It looks like a Laughing Gull, but has a white band between the gray on the wings and the black wingtips. In summer (during the breeding season) the breast is quite rosy and the head is black. (98)

Bonaparte's Gull A tiny gull with a big white patch on the fore-edge of the wing; common locally in many harbors from late summer until spring. In summer the head is black (as shown). This gull looks like a pigeon at rest, but is more often seen in flocks on the wing, flapping like a tern and flashing its white wing patches. (99)

Terns

These birds belong to the gull family but specialize in diving headfirst after fish. In flight, most terns are graceful and quite striking, with their long tail streamers and black and white plumage. In summer they have a prominent black cap and a colorful bill.

Little Tern Our smallest tern. In summer, it has a yellow bill and a white forehead. (100)

Common Tern A black-capped tern with a reddish bill and a deeply forked tail. It is white below and gray above, with blackish wingtips. As in most of the smaller terns, the legs are red (101). Forster's Tern (not shown) is very similar, but its wingtips are whitish (not black). It breeds on inland marshes as well as near the coast.

Royal Tern One of our largest terns. It has a thick orange bill and a black crown, featuring a swept-back crest. (102)

Franklin's Gull

Bonaparte's Gull

Little Tern

Royal Tern

Common Tern

Black Skimmer

Atlantic
Puffin

Rock Dove

Band-tailed
Pigeon

Mourning Dove

Black Skimmer A bizarre bird (related to gulls and terns) that skims the surface of the waves with the elongated lower mandible of its bill. After cutting a line through the water, the skimmer retraces its path to capture any fish that have been attracted to the surface. This bird is black above and white below; the bill is reddish orange with a black tip. (103)

Atlantic Puffin A clown-like sea bird that breeds from Maine northward. It feeds on fish in the cold waters of the North Atlantic. This bird is mostly black above and white below, with bright red webbed feet. Its unusual triangular bill is blue, yellow, and red. (104)

Pigeons and Doves

Within this family, the name pigeon *is used for the larger birds and* dove *is used for the smaller ones. These short-necked birds have short legs and grayish or brownish plumage. They feed on all kinds of seeds, buds, and some fruits. Their cooing calls are very distinctive.*

Rock Dove Sometimes called the Rock Pigeon — the common pigeon of our cities and towns, originally imported from Europe. It is normally bluish gray with some purple on the neck, but sometimes comes in different colors. The feet are red. (105)

Band-tailed Pigeon A large pigeon, common in woodlands of the Rockies and the Pacific Coast. It has a purplish head and breast, gray wings and rump, a white patch on the nape, and a yellow bill. (106)

Mourning Dove A widespread dove, easily recognized by its long pointed tail and uniformly buffy plumage. When they hear the mournful cooing of this bird for the first time, many beginning birders think they have heard an owl. (107)

Cuckoos

Unlike their famous counterparts in Europe, our cuckoos do not say cuckoo (as in a "cuckoo" clock) or lay their eggs in other birds' nests. In summer they hunt for caterpillars in woodlots and often go undetected.

Yellow-billed Cuckoo In this species, the lower mandible of the bill is yellow and the flight feathers are chestnut-colored. The large white spots on the tail feathers are more noticeable from below. (108)

Black-billed Cuckoo Similar to the Yellow-billed Cuckoo (above), but uniformly brownish gray above and with narrow white tips (not large spots) on the tail feathers. In this bird, the entire bill is black. (109)

Greater Roadrunner A long-tailed, brown-streaked bird that runs along dry ground, looking for lizards, snakes, and large insects. This western cuckoo makes a variety of sounds (including clucks, crowing, coos, and a whinny), but it does not say *beep-beep*. It has a shaggy brown crest and a blue and red stripe behind the eye. (110)

Owls

These are chiefly birds of the night that feed on small animals. Their soft, dense plumage allows them to be virtually noiseless in flight. They have remarkable eyesight and excellent hearing, but are best-known for their loud, mournful calls, which ring through the night.

Barn Owl The heart-shaped face and soft buffy upperparts distinguish this superb mouse-catcher. It nests in barns, hollow trees, caves, and sandbanks. (111)

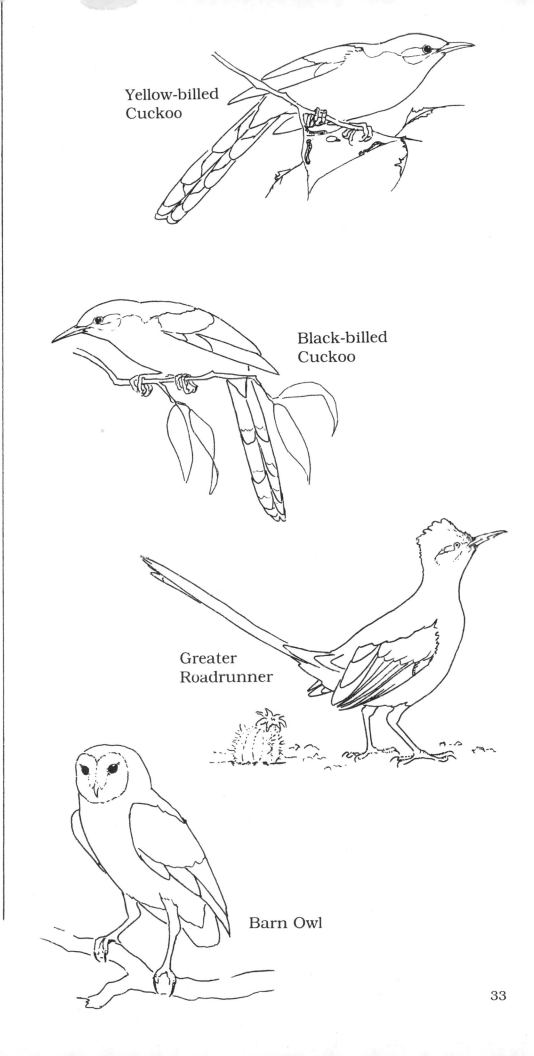

Yellow-billed Cuckoo

Black-billed Cuckoo

Greater Roadrunner

Barn Owl

Common
Screech Owl

Barred Owl

Snowy Owl

Great
Horned Owl

Common
Nighthawk

Common Screech Owl Our most widespread small owl; rarely seen in the daytime. It comes in two color phases — a gray phase and a red phase. Note the ear tufts and the small size of this owl. Look for it in hollows and abandoned woodpecker holes in trees in your neighborhood. (112)

Barred Owl A large owl without ear tufts that lives in deep woods and swamps of the East and South. Its call is often described as *Who cooks for you, who cooks for you-all?* The eyes of this owl are dark brown, not yellow. (113)

Great Horned Owl Our largest owl with ear tufts — roughly eagle-sized. Note the piercing yellow eyes on a chestnut-colored face. This owl eats rabbits, skunks, squirrels, and occasionally smaller owls. (114)

Snowy Owl A large white owl that breeds on the Arctic tundra. In some years when its prey (especially small rodents called lemmings) becomes scarce, this owl comes south for the winter to the salt marshes and plains of our northern states. (115)

Common Nighthawk Not a true hawk at all. This bird spends summer nights in the air, scooping up insects with its large mouth. It is brownish overall, with a white throat and a conspicuous white band near the tip of each wing. It has recently begun to nest on flat city rooftops. (116)

Chimney Swift The "flying cigar" — common all summer in the East, flying over towns and fields. Although this bird looks like a swallow, it cannot perch on wires or tree branches the way swallows do. Instead, it has to cling to vertical surfaces, such as the insides of hollow trees and chimneys. (117)

Ruby-throated Hummingbird The only hummingbird normally found east of the Mississippi R. Both sexes have a glossy green back, crown, and sides, but the female's throat is whitish with very light spots, not ruby-colored. Hummers are the only birds that can fly backwards. (118)

Rufous Hummingbird Common over western mountains and valleys; migrates from as far as Alaska to Guatemala. The male is mostly rufous (rusty brown) overall, but has a white chest and a bright red gorget (throat patch). (119)

Belted Kingfisher A crested kingfisher that plunges beneath the water to seize fish with its long beak. Its loud call is heard rattling over many ponds and rivers. Unlike in most bird species, the female bird (shown) is more colorful than the male, with her chestnut-colored breastband. (120)

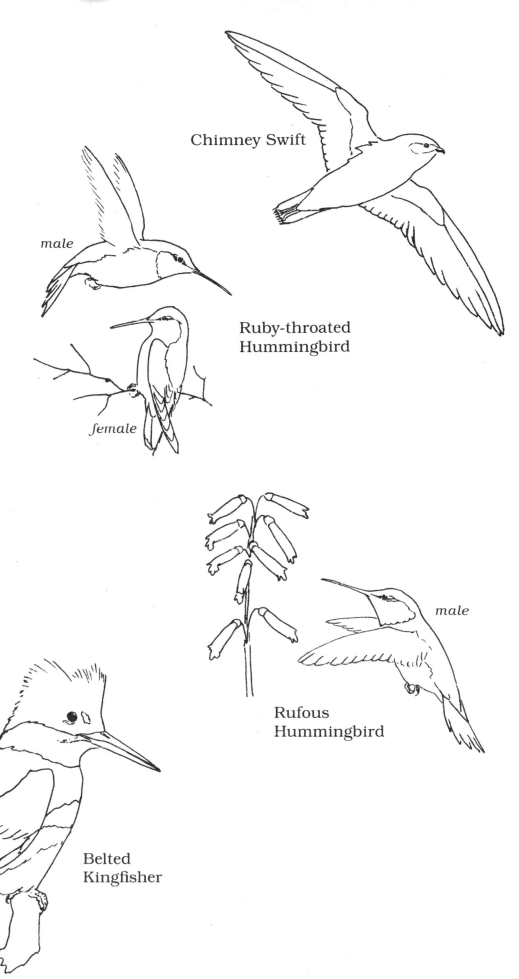

Chimney Swift

male

Ruby-throated Hummingbird

female

Rufous Hummingbird

male

Belted Kingfisher

female

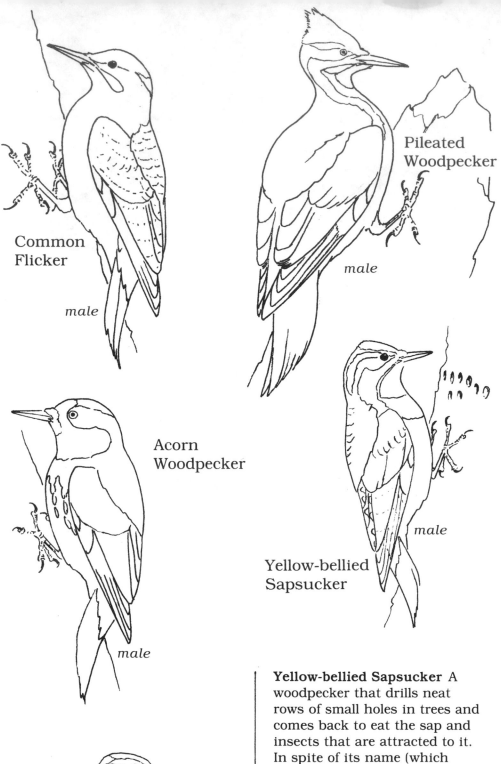

Common Flicker

male

Pileated Woodpecker

male

Acorn Woodpecker

Yellow-bellied Sapsucker

male

male

Hairy Woodpecker

male

Woodpeckers

These birds specialize in digging their prey (insects and grubs) out of wood with their powerful chisel-like bills. They use their strong clawed feet to cling to treetrunks and prop themselves up with their stiff tail feathers. These birds have long narrow tongues that coil back into the skull. In flickers the tongue is barbed and coated with sticky saliva, for lapping up ants and other insects; in sapsuckers it has a brushlike tip, for licking sap. In most woodpeckers the tip of the tongue is sharp and horny, for spearing wood-boring beetles.

Common Flicker A large, uncrested woodpecker with a conspicuous white rump; often seen on the ground feeding on ants as well as in trees. The back is brown with black bars and the breast is buffy with black spots. At least two different races of flickers (formerly thought to be separate species) are found in different parts of North America: In most of the western birds the wings are reddish underneath and the male has a red mustache. The eastern flickers are usually golden yellow under the wings, and the male has a black mustache. (121)

Pileated Woodpecker A huge woodpecker that feeds on wood-boring beetles and carpenter ants in heavily wooded areas. This bird is all black above, with white stripes on the head and neck and a bright red crest. The male also has a bright red mustache. (122)

Acorn Woodpecker A western woodpecker that looks like a clown because of the bold color pattern (black, white, and red) on its face. It usually lives near oak groves, where it stores acorns in thousands of holes drilled in treetrunks or telephone poles. (123)

Yellow-bellied Sapsucker A woodpecker that drills neat rows of small holes in trees and comes back to eat the sap and insects that are attracted to it. In spite of its name (which many non-birders find very amusing), this bird has only a slight yellowish wash or tint on its belly. (124)

Hairy Woodpecker One of our two common small, black and white woodpeckers — larger and less common than the Downy. Compared to the Downy, the Hairy has a larger head, a longer bill, and no black spots on the white outer tail feathers. (125)

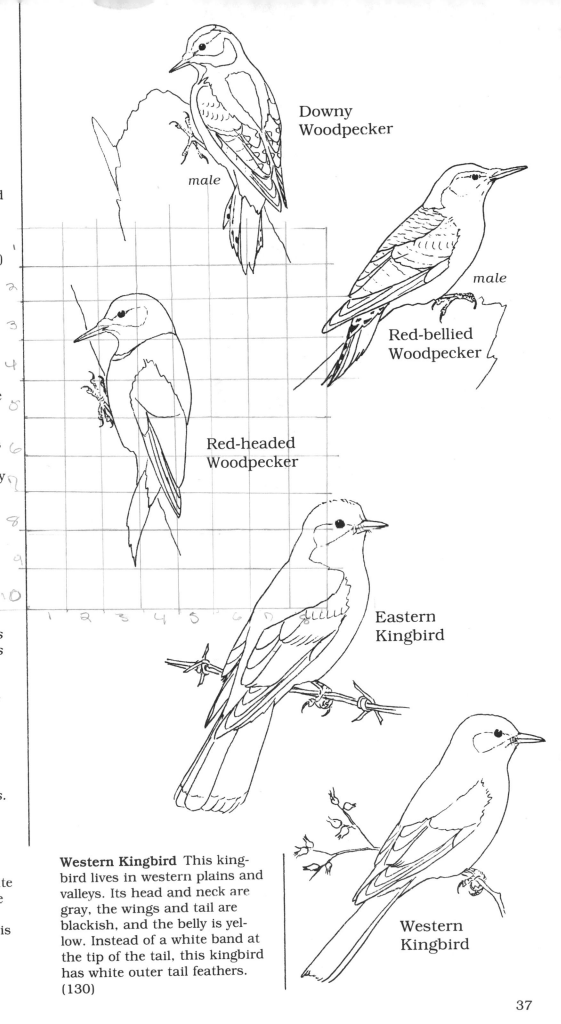

Downy Woodpecker Smaller than the Hairy, with a tiny bill and black spots on the white outer tail feathers. As in the Hairy, the males have some red on the head (which the females lack). (126)

Red-bellied Woodpecker Common in much of the central and southern U.S. The back of this bird is black and white (like a zebra's) and the nape is red in both sexes. In the male (shown) the red patch on the head is larger, extending onto the crown. The name of this woodpecker is misleading, because there is almost no red on its belly. (127)

Red-headed Woodpecker Most common in the Midwest, where it occurs in open areas as well as in woods. Unfortunately, cars kill many of these birds as they fly slowly across roads at bumper height. This is the only eastern woodpecker in which the head is solid red in both sexes. The back is solid black, the rump and belly are white, and the wings are black with large white patches. (128)

Tyrant Flycatchers

With strong wings and bristles around the mouth, these birds are well adapted for catching the thousands of insects they eat. Most of us see flycatchers only in the warmer months, when their prey is abundant. Some of them are attractive birds of roadsides and backyards but many are drab brown birds of the woodlands.

Eastern Kingbird A scrappy bird that will defend its nest and territory in aerial battles with crows and other predators. It is black above and white below, with a distinctive white band at the tip of its tail. The small red patch on the crown is rarely seen. (129)

Western Kingbird This kingbird lives in western plains and valleys. Its head and neck are gray, the wings and tail are blackish, and the belly is yellow. Instead of a white band at the tip of the tail, this kingbird has white outer tail feathers. (130)

Downy Woodpecker

male

Red-bellied Woodpecker

male

Red-headed Woodpecker

Eastern Kingbird

Western Kingbird

37

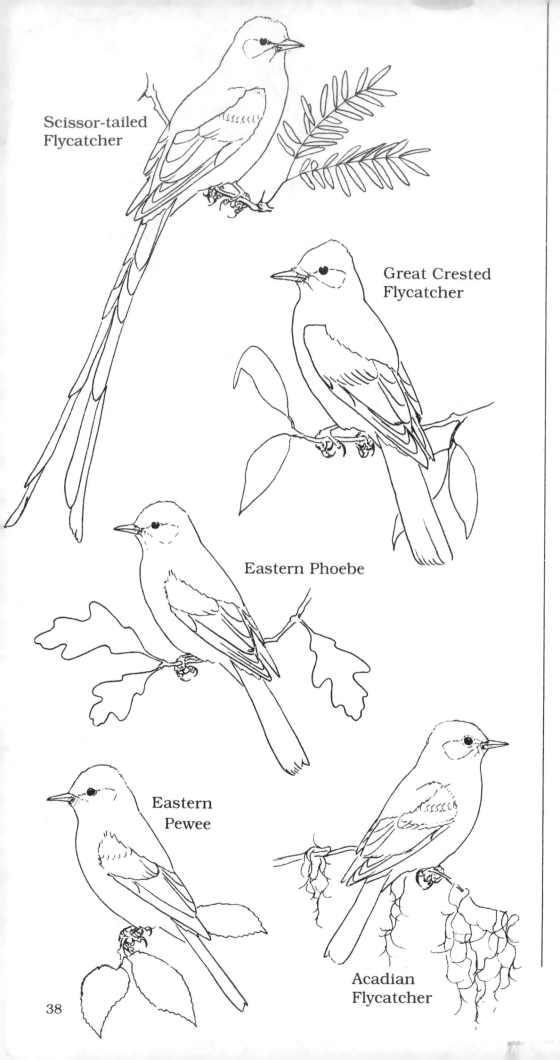

Scissor-tailed
Flycatcher

Great Crested
Flycatcher

Eastern Phoebe

Eastern
Pewee

Acadian
Flycatcher

Scissor-tailed Flycatcher A large flycatcher with very long, forked, black and white tail feathers. It is pale gray with scarlet and rose on the sides. In summer it can be seen on fenceposts and overhead wires from the Great Plains to southern Texas. (131)

Great Crested Flycatcher Spends the summer in our eastern broadleaf forests. A loud, whistled *wheep* calls attention to this grayish brown bird with chestnut-colored wings and tail, and a yellow belly. It often lines its nest with shed snakeskins. (132) In many western woodlands, the **Ash-throated Flycatcher** (which is somewhat smaller and paler) takes the place of this species.

Eastern Phoebe A hardy bird that constantly wags its tail as it searches for insects near bridges, houses, and streams. It is dark brown with a whitish (or yellowish) breast. Its call note is a distinctive *phee-be*. (133)

Empidonax **Flycatchers** North America is home to almost a dozen small flycatchers with a light eye-ring and pale wing-bars. Most of them are drab birds, with no bright colors. The **Acadian Flycatcher** is the common *Empidonax* flycatcher of the Appalachian and southeastern forests. It utters an abrupt *ka-reep* from the lower trees in the forest. (134)

Eastern Pewee Looks like an Eastern Phoebe, but has more prominent wing bars and does not wag its tail. In summer, its slurred whistle (*pee-ah-wee*) can be heard from the treetops in eastern forests. (135)

Olive-sided Flycatcher Whistles *hic, three beers* from the tops of dead trees near clearings in northern and western coniferous forests. The dark olive "vest" ("unbuttoned" down the front, leaving a narrow strip of white down the belly) gives this bird its name. (136)

Vermilion Flycatcher A colorful flycatcher of the Southwest that brightens up the lowlands of Arizona and Texas. The male's brilliant red crown and underparts are most conspicuous during his flight-songs. (137)

Horned Lark (138) (in Winter Field Scene, p. 63)

Swallows

These birds catch insects by the mouthful as they fly low over fields and ponds. They have very weak feet, but often perch in large groups on wires and buildings.

Purple Martin Our largest swallow. It can glide for long periods and feeds on large insects in midair, such as moths, grasshoppers, drone honeybees, and flies. This dark purple swallow lives in colonies, often in special "apartment houses" in backyards. (139)

Tree Swallow A delightful, slow-flying swallow that is pure white below and shiny green or blue above (depending on the light). It readily moves into birdhouses that are free of sparrows and starlings. (140)

Violet-green Swallow Found chiefly in our western mountains and valleys. It is white below, like a Tree Swallow, but has a white eyebrow and a violet rump, with white patches on either side. The crown, back, and wings are green. (141)

Bank Swallow A tiny swallow that is brown above and white below, with a dark breastband. Colonies of these birds nest along rivers and streams, where they dig burrows into the banks. (Sometimes the burrows are several feet long!) (142)

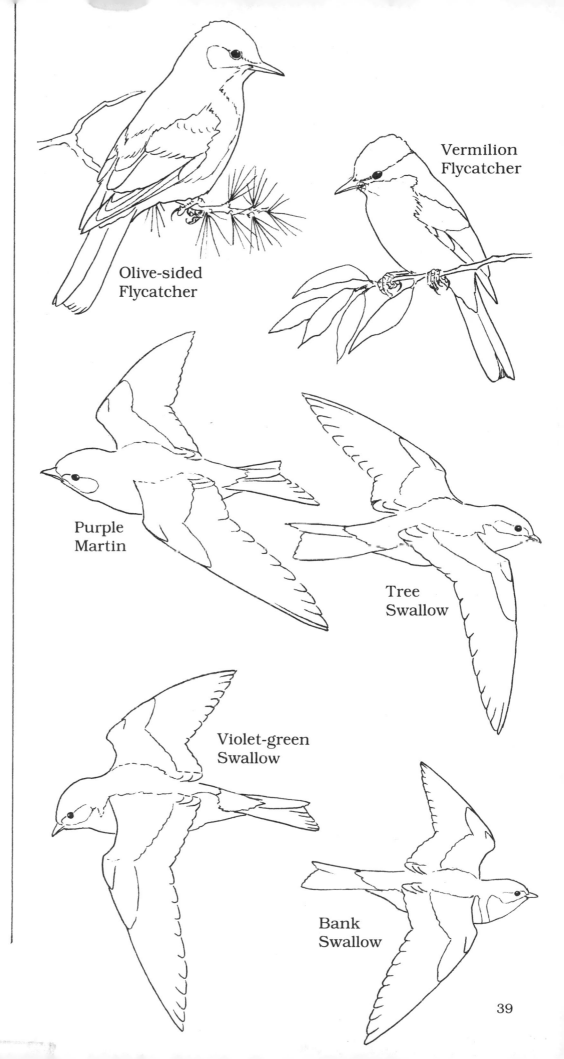

Olive-sided Flycatcher

Vermilion Flycatcher

Purple Martin

Tree Swallow

Violet-green Swallow

Bank Swallow

39

Rough-winged
Swallow

Cliff
Swallow

Barn
Swallow

Gray Jay

Scrub Jay

Steller's
Jay

Rough-winged Swallow Similar to the Bank Swallow (p. 39) in color and feeding habits — both birds often hunt for mosquitoes and other insects over water. The Rough-winged Swallow is larger, however, and has a dusky throat instead of a white one with a dark "necklace." It also prefers to nest alone, rather than in large colonies. (143)

Cliff Swallow The swallow that is famous for returning to San Juan Capistrano each year; found throughout North America in open areas near buildings and cliffs. This swallow builds mud nests in colonies under eaves and bridges. (144)

Barn Swallow Our most common swallow; usually found near farm buildings, where it plasters its mud and grass nests under the eaves and rafters. This fast flier is gorgeous with its dark blue back, rusty orange underparts, and long pointed tail streamers. (front cover, 145)

Crows, Jays, Magpies

This group of well-known birds is actually related to the colorful birds-of-paradise of New Guinea. The birds in this family have strong feet and a stout bill that is usually hooked at the tip.

Gray Jay Also called the Canada Jay or the "camp robber." This pale gray jay with a small bill looks like a huge chickadee. It is found in cool northern forests at higher elevations. (146)

Blue Jay (147) (in Backyard Scene, p. 47)

Scrub Jay Similar to the Blue Jay but without the crest. The wings and tail of this jay are solid blue (with no white markings) and the back is brownish tan. Some birds have short dark streaks across the breast, but not a solid black necklace. (148)

Steller's Jay A large crested jay of our western forests. The wings, tail, and belly are dark blue with no white spots; the head, upper back, and breast are black. (149)

Black-billed Magpie Magpies are jay-like birds of the western U.S. They are quite attractive with their long, glossy greenish tails and their bold black and white wings and body (150a). In central California, the **Yellow-billed Magpie** (see close-up of head) takes the place of this magpie. (150b)

Clark's Nutcracker A crestless jay of the western forests, found at high elevations near the tree line. It is gray with white patches on its black wings and tail. It eats cedar and juniper berries, along with pine seeds and acorns, which it cracks open with its bill. (151)

American Crow A very familiar bird in most parts of the U.S. and Canada. The noisy *caw, caw* of this large black bird can be heard in cities and suburbs as well as on farms. (152)

Chickadees, Titmice

These familiar small birds roam our woodlands in small groups, searching for insects. They often visit bird feeders in winter and seem to have little fear of humans.

Black-capped Chickadee Not the only chickadee with a black cap and bib — look for a white wing patch and rusty sides to confirm your identification of this one. The pleasing *chick-a-dee-dee-dee* call of this bird is easily recognized by everyone who loves the woods of the northern U.S. and Canada. (153)

Carolina Chickadee Similar to the Black-capped Chickadee, but with solid gray wings and a faster, higher-pitched call (*chick-a-tsee-dee, tsee-dee*). This species takes the place of the Black-cap in southeastern forests, south of N.J. and Ohio. (154)

Mountain Chickadee A western chickadee, found in mountain forests from southwestern Canada to the southwestern U.S. It has a distinctive white "eyebrow" on its black cap. (155)

Yellow-billed Magpie

Black-billed Magpie

Clark's Nutcracker

American Crow

Black-capped Chickadee

Mountain Chickadee

Carolina Chickadee

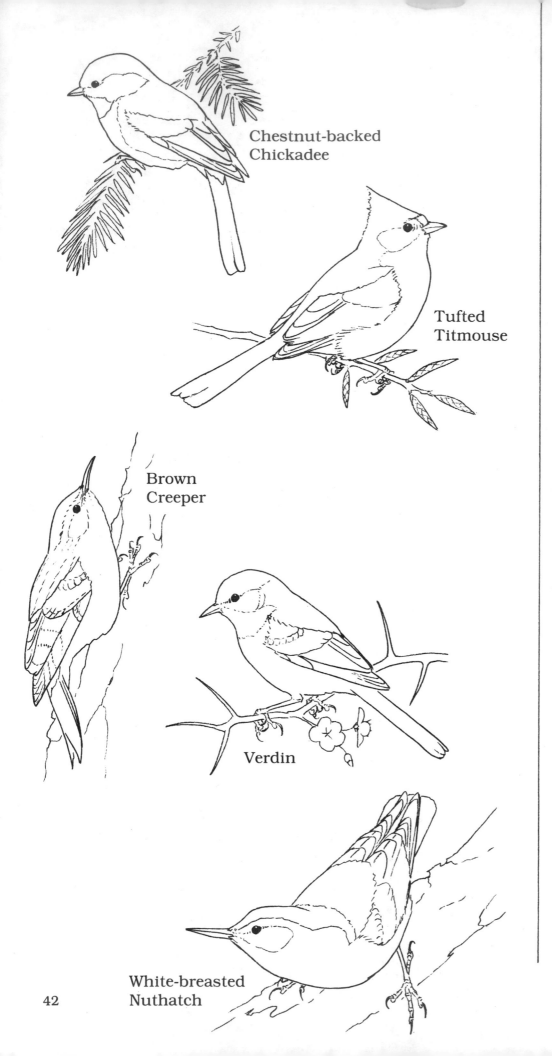

Chestnut-backed
Chickadee

Tufted
Titmouse

Brown
Creeper

Verdin

White-breasted
Nuthatch

Chestnut-backed Chickadee
An attractive bird that looks
like other chickadees except for
its chestnut back and sides. It
lives in redwoods and other
giant conifers and hardwoods
in the wet forests of the Pacific
Coast. Its call is a hoarse *tseek-
see-see*. (156)

Tufted Titmouse "A chickadee
with a crest" — common in forests and at bird feeders in the
eastern U.S. It is gray above
and white below, with rusty
sides. Its most common call
(which can be heard year-
round) is a whistle that sounds
like *peter, peter, peter, peter*.
(157)

Verdin A small gray bird (like a
chickadee) with a yellow head
and chestnut shoulders. It lives
in mesquite thickets and
among cacti in southwestern
deserts, where it searches for
insects, berries, and nectar.
(158)

Brown Creeper A well-camou-
flaged, brown-streaked bird
that looks like a piece of bark
as it spirals up thick treetrunks. Like a miniature woodpecker, it props itself up with
its stiff tail feathers and probes
for insects under the bark with
its thin, down-curved bill. Its
high-pitched call note is a single *seee*. (159)

White-breasted Nuthatch
Nuthatches are small birds that
carefully search for insects as
they go down treetrunks headfirst. The call of this nuthatch
is a loud *yank-yank*. Its back
is blue and its underparts are
white (except for the rusty
patch under the rump). The
male has a black cap above a
solid white face. (160)

Red-breasted Nuthatch A small
northern nuthatch that lives
chiefly in coniferous forests. It
is blue above and rusty orange
below, with black and white eye
stripes (in both sexes) and a

black cap (in the male). This bird's call sounds like a tin horn: *ank-ank-ank-ank-ank*. (161)

North American Dipper A starling-shaped bird that lives in fast-flowing streams of the Rockies, Sierras, and Pacific Coast mountain ranges. It bobs and dives into the water and often walks on the bottom as it searches for insect larvae and small fish. This unusual bird is gray overall, with yellow legs. (162)

Wrens

These small brownish birds are often seen perching with their tails cocked up. Most of them are superb songsters. They have slender curved bills that are well adapted for probing crevices for insects and spiders. As you might expect in birds that spend most of their time in the undergrowth (or on stone walls), the wings are relatively weak and the legs are strong.

House Wren A lively little brown bird with a cheery bubbling song that rises and falls. Unlike most wrens, this bird will nest in backyard bird houses as well as in tree hollows (such as abandoned woodpecker holes) near clearings in forests. (163)

Carolina Wren A large wren found in thickets in the eastern U.S. It calls *tea-kettle, tea-kettle, tea-kettle* all year long. It is buff below and a warm rusty brown above, with a long white eyebrow. (164)

Mockingbirds and Thrashers

This group of talented songsters and mimics includes mockingbirds, thrashers, and catbirds. All of them have long

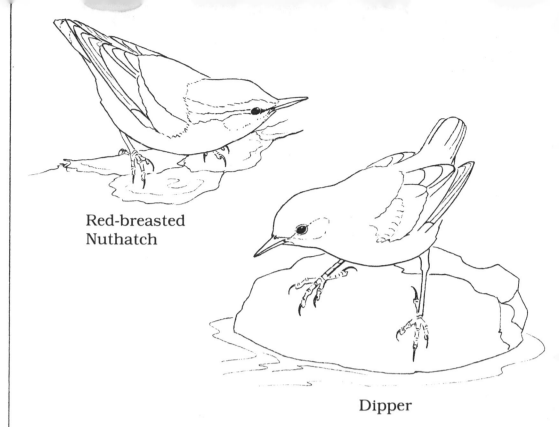

Red-breasted Nuthatch

Dipper

House Wren

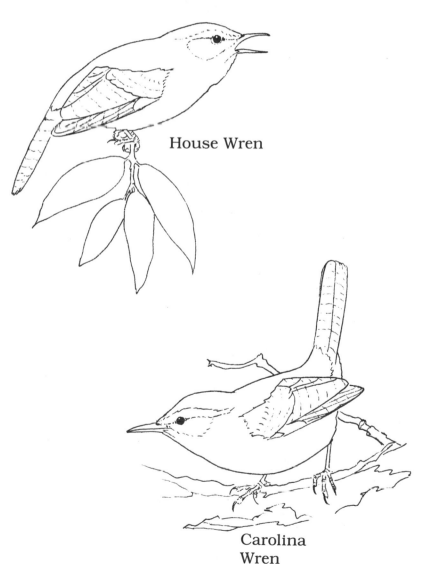

Carolina Wren

Gray
Catbird

California
Thrasher

Brown
Thrasher

Varied Thrush

Wood
Thrush

tails and short wings. In most species (except the mocking-bird) the bill curves slightly downward. These birds eat insects, berries, and other fruit and are often seen on the ground.

Northern Mockingbird (165) (in Backyard Scene, p. 47)

Gray Catbird Also a mimic, but does not repeat songs over and over the way the mockingbird does. This bird also makes its own catlike *mewing* sounds. It lives in thickets and suburban gardens throughout most of the U.S. (except the Southwest). The catbird is dark gray with a black cap and has an inconspicuous patch of chestnut under its tail. (166)

Brown Thrasher Much larger than a thrush (p. 45), with yellow eyes and a long, down-curved bill. This bird is a rich rusty brown above, with brown stripes on the breast. It utters a variety of calls (including a harsh *chack!*) from woods and thickets. (167)

California Thrasher An unspotted thrasher that lives on the West Coast. It is dark brown with a pale cinnamon belly, and — unlike the Brown Towhee, which shares its range — has a slender, down-curved bill and a blackish stripe below the eye. (168)

Thrushes

Our finest songsters. This family includes the American Robin — the most familiar bird in North America. Many of our other thrushes are shy brownish birds of the forest. Although some live in trees and feed on berries, most thrushes run across lawns or the forest floor.

American Robin (169) (in Backyard Scene, p. 47)

Varied Thrush A thrush of dense forests in the Northwest that is increasingly straying eastward in winter to backyard bird feeders. The male looks like a male Robin but has a broad black band on the breast, an orange eyestripe, and orange wing bars. (170)

Wood Thrush A large thrush with a reddish back and a white breast, which is peppered with many large black spots. It sings a beautiful flutelike *ee-oo-lay* from the depths of eastern forests. (171)

Hermit Thrush A small thrush with perhaps the most ethereal, varied song of all. It is brown above, with a reddish tail and a moderate sprinkling of brown spots on the chest. (172)

Swainson's Thrush The least rusty of our common thrushes. It is gray-brown above and has brown spots on its breast like a Hermit, but its tail is brown and it has a conspicuous buffy ring around each eye. This thrush often feeds on berries in trees and shrubs. (173)

Eastern Bluebird A beautiful small thrush that used to be more common in the East, but has suffered from the use of pesticides and from competition with other, more aggressive birds (starlings and House Sparrows) for nesting places. The male (shown) is a bright blue bird with a rusty breast and a white belly. As in all bluebirds, the female is duller (more grayish). (174)

Western Bluebird A similar bluebird of the western woodlands. In this species the male (shown) has a rusty patch on his back and a completely blue throat. (175)

Mountain Bluebird Another western bluebird that is soft peacock-blue all over, with no orange coloring. It likes open country with a few trees nearby for nesting. It catches insects on the ground in summer and feeds on fruit in winter. (176)

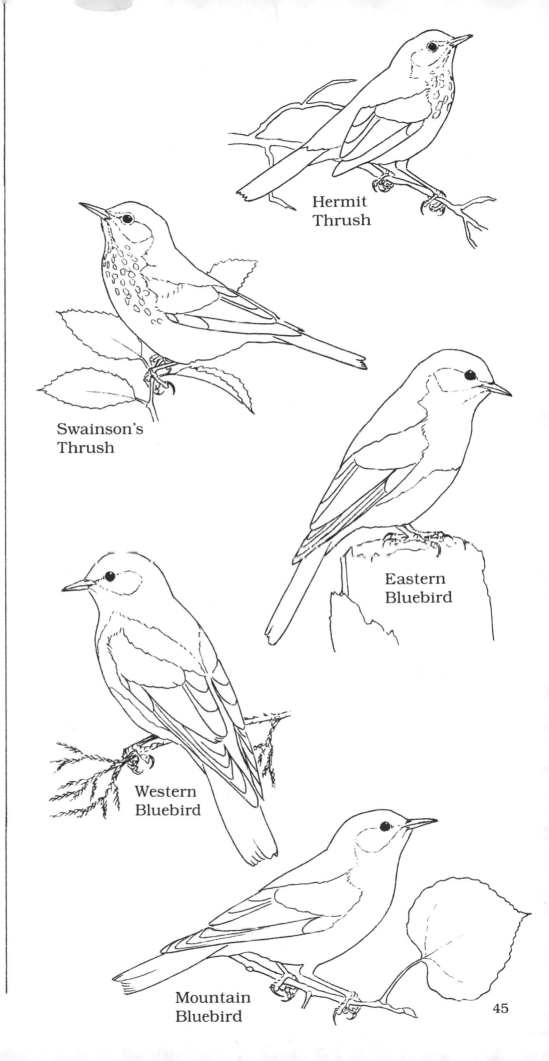

Hermit Thrush

Swainson's Thrush

Eastern Bluebird

Western Bluebird

Mountain Bluebird

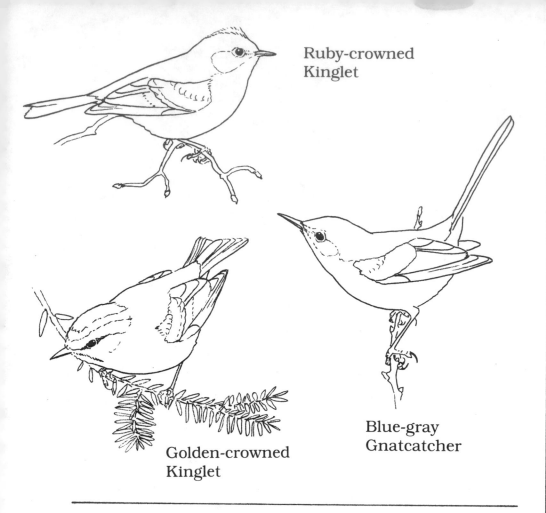

Ruby-crowned
Kinglet

Golden-crowned
Kinglet

Blue-gray
Gnatcatcher

Kinglets and Gnatcatchers

Kinglets are tiny, active, warblerlike birds with brightly colored crowns and short tails. Gnatcatchers are small gray birds with white feathers on the outer edges of their long tails. They look like miniature mockingbirds. Both of these groups of birds have evolved from a Eurasian group of birds, the Old World warblers.

Blue-gray Gnatcatcher A small bluish gray bird with a white eye-ring and white outer tail feathers. It utters a very high note from tall trees and thickets in our woodlands. This species is expanding its range northward in the U.S. and Canada. (177)

Ruby-crowned Kinglet A common bird with a surprisingly loud song for its size. It has no black stripes on the head. The male rarely shows his ruby crown patch, but often flicks his yellow-edged wings. Note the white ring around the eye (in both sexes). (178)

Golden-crowned Kinglet A northern kinglet with heavy black stripes on the head. The male sometimes shows his reddish crown patch, which is surrounded by yellow. The female's crown is solid yellow. (179)

Northern Oriole (227a) (p. 57)

Northern Cardinal The male is the well-known, all-red bird with a red crest, black face, and thick red-orange beak. The female also has a crest but is brownish orange. The cardinal is now common in suburbs and on farms in much of the East and Southwest. (233)

Backyard Scene

Once you begin to notice the richness of the birdlife around you, you may be surprised at how many birds actually come to visit your neighborhood. Many birders keep a "yard list" of all the birds that come onto their property and are amazed at how many kinds they see. Check your trees during fall and spring migration; scan the skies when hawks, ducks, and geese are on the move; keep your bird feeder full; and look for the source of any new songs you hear.

Blue Jay A lively, noisy bird, abundant in eastern forests (and at bird feeders) and as far west as Alberta and Colorado. It is actually several shades of blue, with a distinctive crest and a black necklace contrasting with its white breast. It eats acorns and beechnuts and buries many of them for later use. (147)

Northern Mockingbird Our most versatile mimic. This bird will sing for hours in thickets, treetops, and on rooftops, imitating a wide variety of other birds' songs. It is a robin-sized bird with a short straight bill. Mostly gray, it has large white and black patches on its wings and tail (which are more visible in flight). (165)

American Robin Perhaps our best-loved bird. It combines beauty, tameness, interesting habits, and a beautiful song. The reddish orange breast, gray back, blackish head and tail, and yellow bill of this bird are well-known to all. (169)

European Starling A native of Europe that was imported into the U.S. less than 100 years ago and may now be the most common resident bird in North America. It is a fine mimic and is very social. This short-tailed bird with a yellow bill is glossy black for most of the year, but becomes spotted in fall and winter. (182)

Backyard Scene

147

227a

165

182

169

233

♀

♂

47

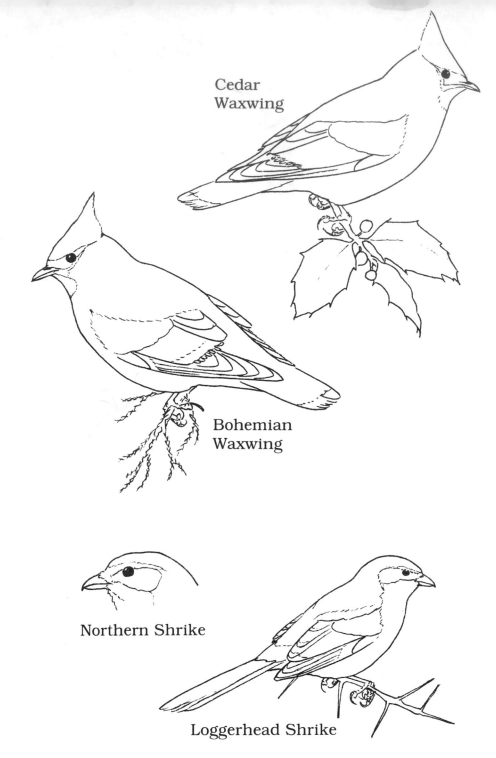

Cedar
Waxwing

Bohemian
Waxwing

Northern Shrike

Loggerhead Shrike

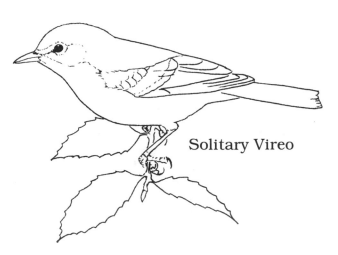

Solitary Vireo

Waxwings

These sleek, berry-eating birds have black and white faces and large crests. They come in soft pastel colors (grayish browns) that are accented by the yellow tips on their tails and the unusual red, waxlike tips on some of their wing feathers (secondaries).

Cedar Waxwing The more common waxwing, with no white on its wings (unlike the Bohemian Waxwing). It has a warm buffy chest, a yellow belly, and a whitish patch under its tail. (180

Bohemian Waxwing A northern and western waxwing. It is entirely gray below, except for the area below its rump, which is a deep reddish brown. It has large white bars on its wings. (181

Loggerhead Shrike A shrike looks like a mockingbird with a black "Lone Ranger" mask and a long, hooked beak (see close-up of head). Shrikes perch conspicuously on tree branches and overhead wires, searching for large insects and small birds to eat. (183)

Vireos

These birds are quite common in summer in many of our forests and woodlands, yet many people are unaware of them because they are less active than warblers. They are also relatively drab, which makes them even more inconspicuous among the leaves. You are more likely to notice them because of their loud, repetitious songs. Vireos have a slightly hooked tip at the end of the bill and eye-rings or eye-stripes.

Solitary Vireo A large vireo with white wing bars and eye-rings ("spectacles"). Eastern birds have a gray head, a greenish back, and yellow sides; western ones are all gray above. Both races are white below. (184)

Red-eyed Vireo One of the most abundant birds of the eastern forests in summer. This small bird can be heard calling *cheery-up, cheery-oop* hundreds of times a day in the treetops. It has a gray cap, a black and white eyebrow over its red eye, a green back, and a white breast. (185)

Warbling Vireo A drab gray vireo that gets its name from its song. (It actually sounds more like a Purple Finch than a warbler.) It is the same size as the Red-eyed Vireo and has a white eyestripe over its dark eye. (186)

Warblers

The most colorful and entertaining family of North American birds. These tiny insect-eaters come in a whole rainbow of colors and patterns: red, orange, yellow, green, and blue, with black and white accents. The birds shown here are breeding males, in their colorful spring plumage. In fall they are much duller and are very hard to tell apart.

Black-and-white Warbler A warbler that acts like a nuthatch, going up and down tree-trunks and large branches. It is black and white all over. (187)

Prothonotary Warbler A large unstriped warbler of southeastern wooded swamps. It has a golden yellow (almost orange) head and breast and a solid grayish back. The wings and tail are blue-gray, with no bars. (188)

Golden-winged Warbler An unstriped warbler that breeds in the northeastern U.S. and often hybridizes with the Blue-winged Warbler (below). This bird has a yellow crown as well as a golden yellow patch on the wing (which gives this species its name). It is gray above and white below, with a black patch on the face and throat that is divided by a white stripe. (189)

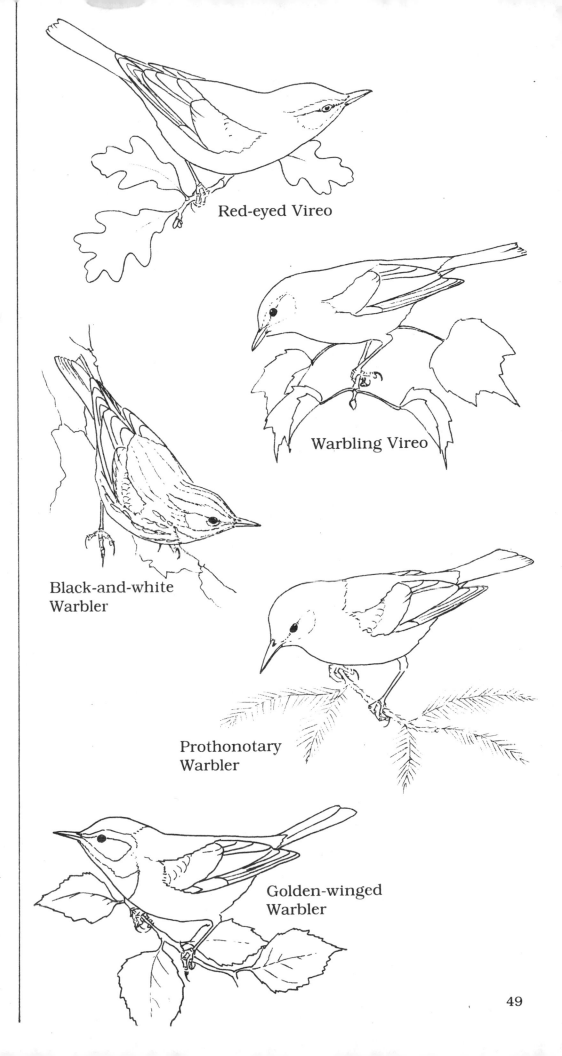

Red-eyed Vireo

Warbling Vireo

Black-and-white Warbler

Prothonotary Warbler

Golden-winged Warbler

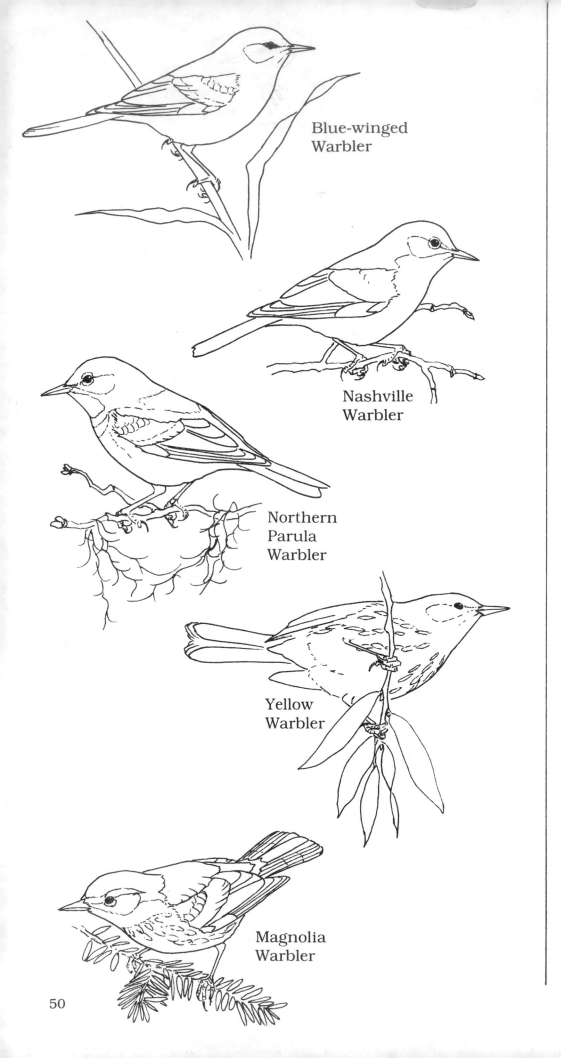

Blue-winged
Warbler

Nashville
Warbler

Northern
Parula
Warbler

Yellow
Warbler

Magnolia
Warbler

Blue-winged Warbler An un-striped warbler that lives at the edge of eastern forests. It is mostly yellow, with an olive back, bluish gray wings (with two white wing bars), and a gray tail. Note the narrow black stripe through the eye. (190)

Nashville Warbler A tree-dweller, found near woodland edges throughout the northern and eastern U.S. It is clear yellow below and greenish above, with a gray head. Note the white eye-ring ("spectacles"). (191)

Northern Parula Warbler Our smallest warbler. Its buzzy, ascending trill can be heard in many eastern forests, particularly those that have moss hanging near water. This warbler is blue-gray above with an olive back and white wing bars. Both sexes have a yellow throat, a yellow breast, and a white belly, but the male has a dark chestnut band across his chest. (192)

Yellow Warbler A brilliant yellow warbler, found in open shrubs and bushes near water. The male has reddish brown (rusty) streaks on the breast. If a cowbird lays an egg in the nest of this warbler, the female Yellow Warbler usually builds a new nest on top and starts again. (193)

Magnolia Warbler A black and yellow warbler that can be seen in magnolias during migration. It breeds in young conifers from Massachusetts and Michigan north. This warbler looks like some Yellow-rumped Warblers (the Myrtle race — see below) but it has a black band at the end of its tail. The Magnolia's underparts are yellow (not white) with black streaks. (194)

Cape May Warbler A warbler that breeds mainly in Canada but is often found on the Atlantic Coast during fall migration. It is yellow with an olive back, dark streaks on the back and breast, and a large white patch on the olive wings. The male has a chestnut face patch. (195)

Black-throated Blue Warbler An unstriped warbler that lives in the undergrowth of eastern woodlands. The male is blue above, with a black throat and sides that contrast with the white parts below. Both sexes have a small white wing patch (less conspicuous in the female), which is sometimes referred to as a "pocket handkerchief." (196)

Black-throated Gray Warbler A striped warbler that feeds in the undergrowth of western forests, and in smaller trees (such as oaks, pines, and junipers) or chaparral (brush). It is black and white all over, with a gray back and a small yellow spot in front of the eye. (197)

Yellow-rumped Warbler A common warbler that comes in two color patterns, which are now considered different races within the same species (see below). This warbler flies out to catch insects in midair and gleans them from leaves on trees. In the **Myrtle race**, found east of the Rockies, the breeding male has a blacker head and a white throat (198a). In **Audubon's race** (the western form), the breeding male has a gray head, a yellow throat, and a wide white patch (not just thin bars) on the wings (198b). Both races have the distinctive yellow rump, the yellow patch on the crown, and the yellow patch at the front of the wings.

Townsend's Warbler A western warbler that breeds in forests from the Pacific Northwest north to Alaska. It looks like a Black-throated Gray Warbler, but is yellow (instead of white) on the head and breast. Note the distinctive black cheek patch, which is surrounded by yellow. (199)

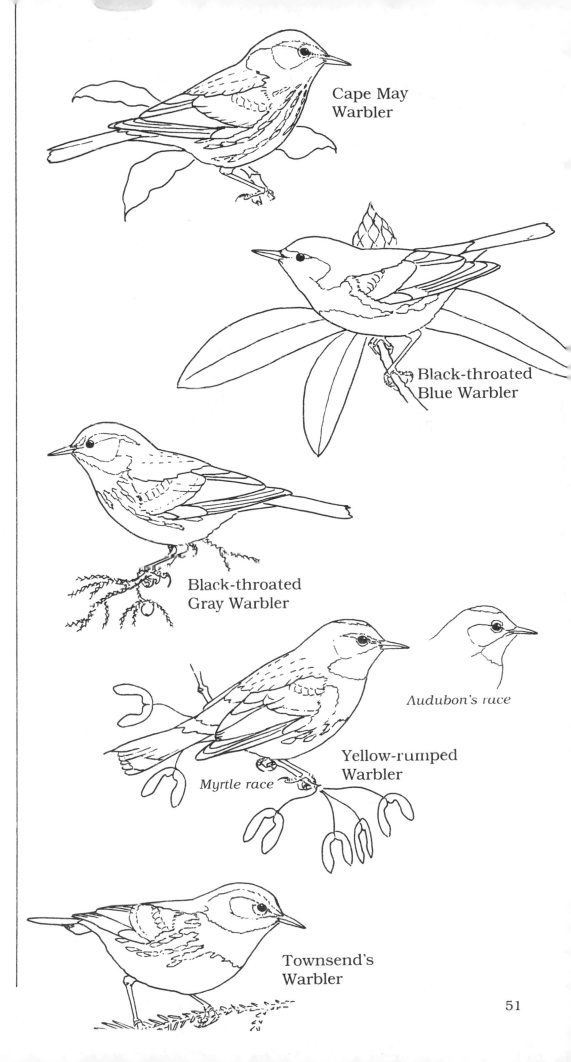

Cape May Warbler

Black-throated Blue Warbler

Black-throated Gray Warbler

Audubon's race

Yellow-rumped Warbler

Myrtle race

Townsend's Warbler

51

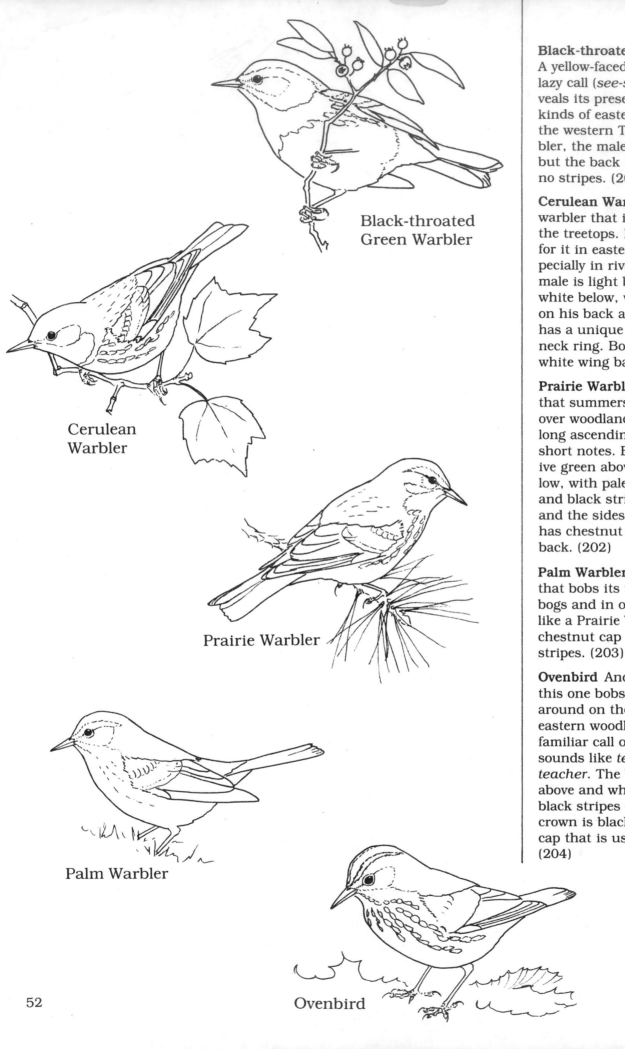

Black-throated Green Warbler A yellow-faced warbler with a lazy call (*see-see-su-sy*) that reveals its presence in many kinds of eastern forests. As in the western Townsend's Warbler, the male's throat is black but the back is olive green with no stripes. (200)

Cerulean Warbler A light blue warbler that is hard to see in the treetops. Look and listen for it in eastern woodlands, especially in river valleys. The male is light blue above and white below, with dark stripes on his back and sides. He also has a unique dark blue or black neck ring. Both sexes have two white wing bars. (201)

Prairie Warbler A tail-wagger that summers in brushy, cut-over woodlands. Its song is a long ascending series of many short notes. Both sexes are olive green above and yellow below, with pale yellow wing bars and black stripes on the head and the sides. The male also has chestnut stripes on his back. (202)

Palm Warbler Another warbler that bobs its tail; found near bogs and in open fields. It looks like a Prairie Warbler but has a chestnut cap and fewer, weaker stripes. (203)

Ovenbird Another tail-wagger; this one bobs its tail as it walks around on the ground in our eastern woodlands. The loud, familiar call of this warbler sounds like *teacher, teacher, teacher*. The bird is olive brown above and white below, with black stripes on the breast. Its crown is black, with an orange cap that is usually concealed. (204)

Black-throated
Green Warbler

Cerulean
Warbler

Prairie Warbler

Palm Warbler

Ovenbird

Waterthrushes are sparrow-sized warblers that are found near streams (usually in wooded areas) and in freshwater bogs. These small, brown-streaked birds look a bit like sparrows, but they walk (instead of hop), often wag their tails, and have very thin bills. The **Northern Waterthrush** breeds in the northern U.S. and Canada and has a beautiful liquid song. Note the buffy eyestripe and underparts and the streaks on the throat. (205)

Hooded Warbler Another unstriped warbler, found in the undergrowth of our southern and eastern forests. This one is quite large and is named for the black hood surrounding its yellow face (in the male). The back is olive green and the underparts are yellow in both sexes. (206)

Blackburnian Warbler A black, white, and orange warbler that nests in northeastern and Canadian forests with tall conifers. The male has an orange-yellow eyestripe and cap and a bright orange throat; the female is duller (more yellow). (207)

Yellow-throated Warbler One of many warblers with a yellow throat. This one has a blue-gray back, a white eyebrow above the black patch on its face, and black stripes on its sides. It lives in southeastern woodlands, especially those with sycamores and cypresses. (208)

Chestnut-sided Warbler A beautiful warbler, abundant in new-growth woodlands and brushy pastures in the eastern U.S. It sings *please, please, pleased to meet-cha*, and is easily identified by its yellow crown and chestnut sides. Its back is yellow green with dark stripes and its underparts and "cheeks" are white. (209)

Northern
Waterthrush

Hooded
Warbler

Blackburnian
Warbler

Yellow-throated
Warbler

Chestnut-sided
Warbler

53

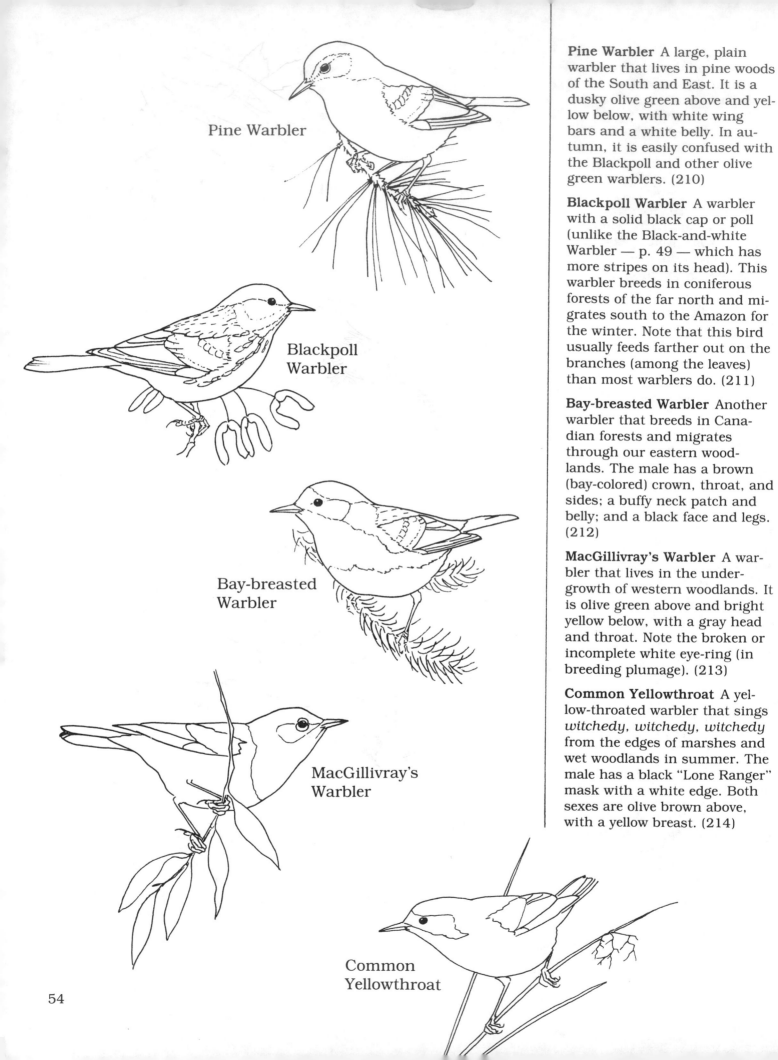

Pine Warbler A large, plain warbler that lives in pine woods of the South and East. It is a dusky olive green above and yellow below, with white wing bars and a white belly. In autumn, it is easily confused with the Blackpoll and other olive green warblers. (210)

Blackpoll Warbler A warbler with a solid black cap or poll (unlike the Black-and-white Warbler — p. 49 — which has more stripes on its head). This warbler breeds in coniferous forests of the far north and migrates south to the Amazon for the winter. Note that this bird usually feeds farther out on the branches (among the leaves) than most warblers do. (211)

Bay-breasted Warbler Another warbler that breeds in Canadian forests and migrates through our eastern woodlands. The male has a brown (bay-colored) crown, throat, and sides; a buffy neck patch and belly; and a black face and legs. (212)

MacGillivray's Warbler A warbler that lives in the undergrowth of western woodlands. It is olive green above and bright yellow below, with a gray head and throat. Note the broken or incomplete white eye-ring (in breeding plumage). (213)

Common Yellowthroat A yellow-throated warbler that sings *witchedy, witchedy, witchedy* from the edges of marshes and wet woodlands in summer. The male has a black "Lone Ranger" mask with a white edge. Both sexes are olive brown above, with a yellow breast. (214)

Pine Warbler

Blackpoll Warbler

Bay-breasted Warbler

MacGillivray's Warbler

Common Yellowthroat

Yellow-breasted Chat Our largest warbler (7″ long). It looks like a giant Yellowthroat, but has a much smaller black mask and a shorter white eyebrow. This bird also has a white eye-ring. It makes a variety of squeaks and whistles from dense shrubs and vines. (215)

Canada Warbler The warbler that wears a "necklace of dark pearls" on its yellow throat. It breeds in Canada, New England, and farther south (along the Appalachian Mt. ridges). Both sexes are solid gray above and yellow below, with a yellow eye-ring. (216)

American Redstart A striking warbler that constantly fans out its tail and flits its wings, like a butterfly. It is found in woodlands west to the Rockies. The male (shown) is a black bird with orange patches on his wings, chest, and tail. As usual, the female is much less conspicuous, with a gray back and yellow patches on the wings and tail. (217)

Painted Redstart A gorgeous bird, found in forested canyons and mountains from west Texas to Arizona. Aside from the bright scarlet breast, this warbler is mostly black with a white wing patch and white outer tail feathers. (218)

House Sparrow It's a fair bet that you could color this bird correctly just by looking out your window. Like the starling, this bird (a weaver finch, not a true sparrow) was imported from Europe and is now found all over North America. The male has a chestnut patch behind the eye and a black throat. (219)

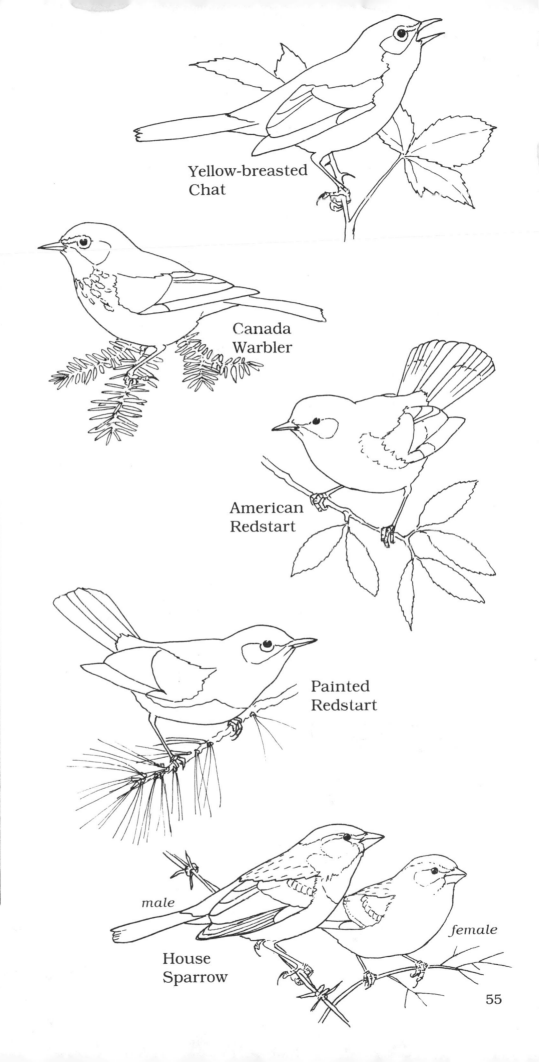

Yellow-breasted
Chat

Canada
Warbler

American
Redstart

Painted
Redstart

male

female

House
Sparrow

55

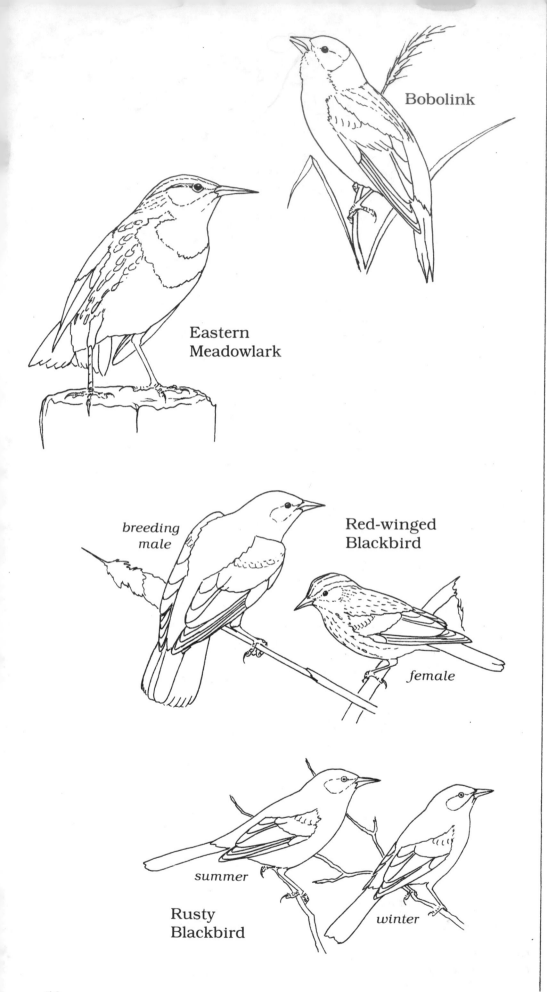

Bobolink

Eastern
Meadowlark

breeding
male

Red-winged
Blackbird

female

Rusty
Blackbird

summer

winter

Blackbirds and their Relatives

This diverse family includes blackbirds, orioles, meadowlarks, and many other well-known birds. They all have a sharply pointed, cone-shaped bill. Many of them travel in flocks in winter and roost together in large numbers.

Bobolink A grassland bird with a nice long burbling song. Note the male's solid black underparts. In breeding plumage, his head, breast, and belly are black, but his nape is yellow and his shoulders and rump are white. In winter, he is brownish with dark streaks, like the female Bobolink. (220)

Meadowlark (Eastern and Western) Another grassland dweller. In spite of their name, these birds belong to the black-bird family, not the lark family. Both the eastern and western species have a distinctive V-shaped bib on the yellow throat and breast. The head and back are streaked with brown and the outer tail feathers (which are more visible in flight) are white. (221)

Red-winged Blackbird One of the first birds to migrate north in early spring. With his bright red and yellow shoulder patches, the black male is quite conspicuous in breeding season, especially when he sings *konk-ah-ree* from exposed perches near marshes and farms. The female is much more drab (brownish). (222)

Rusty Blackbird The male Rusty is a glossy black bird that is rusty only in winter. (The female is black all year round.) The eye is pale yellow in both sexes. This blackbird lives in wooded swamps and grainfields. (223) The male **Brewer's Blackbird** (not shown) is very similar to the male Rusty in summer, but usually has more purplish reflections on his head. He also looks a bit like a cowbird or a grackle, but has a thinner bill and a flatter tail (without the keel — see below).

Common Grackle Found almost everywhere east of the Rockies — also known as the Eastern Grackle. This bird can be recognized by its long tail, which dips down in the middle, like the keel of a boat. The male's shiny black feathers are often highlighted with bronze or purplish reflections. (224)

Yellow-headed Blackbird A large blackbird that nests in noisy colonies in western and midwestern marshes. The male has a yellow head and breast, and a white wing patch (which is more noticeable in flight). (225)

Brown-headed Cowbird A parasitic bird that never makes a nest or raises its own young. The female deposits her eggs in nests of other small birds (such as warblers) that rear the young cowbirds when they hatch. The female cowbird is all gray-brown; the male has a glossy green body and a brown head. The beak is thick in all cowbirds. (226)

Northern Oriole During the last Ice Age, two separate populations of this species were isolated in the East and West. Now that their ranges are expanding and overlapping, some of the eastern and western birds are breeding with each other, causing a mixup, with many hybrids. The **Baltimore race** (227a) lives in eastern forests and near shady lanes. In this eastern form, the male has a solid black head, a brilliant orange breast, and yellow feathers in his tail. **Bullock's race** (227b) is the western form of the Northern Oriole. The male has a black bib and cap, but the orange extends onto his "cheeks." He also has an orange eyebrow and a large white wing patch.

Orchard Oriole A small oriole that looks like a "Baltimore" Oriole with a black tail and dark chestnut underparts (in the male). It lives in eastern orchards, shade trees, and near woodland edges. (228)

Common Grackle

Yellow-headed Blackbird

Brown-headed Cowbird

female

male

"Bullock's" race male

Northern Oriole

"Baltimore" race male

Orchard Oriole

Hooded Oriole

Western Tanager

Scarlet Tanager

Summer Tanager

Hooded Oriole A southwestern oriole that lives in shade trees in towns, in thickets, and in open woods along river bottoms. The face, throat, back, wings, and tail of the male are black; the orange "hood" extends from his crown onto his breast. The male's rump is also orange. (229)

Tanagers

These colorful birds are related to finches. They have long, thick beaks and feed on both insects and fruit.

Western Tanager Found in forests from the Rockies westward. This tanager is yellow with a red head, white wing bars, and a black back, tail, and wings. (230)

Scarlet Tanager The male is all bright red or scarlet, with contrasting solid black wings and tail. He sings like a hoarse Robin from broadleaved trees (such as oaks) in eastern woodlands. The female is greenish yellow. (231)

Summer Tanager The male is rosy red all year, with no crest and no black wings or tail. The female is yellow-green. This tanager breeds in open woodlands in the Southeast and Southwest. Its song is nicer than the Scarlet Tanager's, and its call note is *tricky-dicky.* (232)

Finches

Several subfamilies of birds (such as grosbeaks, sparrows, and buntings) are included in the finch family. Most feed on seeds, insects (particularly in summer), and berries, and have thick beaks that are specialized for cracking seeds.

Northern Cardinal (233) (in Backyard Scene, p. 47)

Pyrrhuloxia A cardinal that lives in deserts and along streams in the Southwest. The male is gray with a red crest, throat, wings and tail. In this cardinal, the thick beak is yellow. (234)

Rose-breasted Grosbeak A fat-billed finch that is common in summer in eastern forests. It sounds like a robin when it sings. The male is a black and white bird with a black head and a rosy patch (shaped like a triangle) on the chest. (235)

Black-headed Grosbeak A relative of the Rose-breasted Grosbeak that lives in western forests. In this species the male is completely orange below, except for the yellow in the middle of his belly. (236)

Blue Grosbeak A grosbeak that is found on farms (especially in fields full of weeds) in most of the southern U.S. This bird looks like a large Indigo Bunting with rusty wing bars. (237)

Indigo Bunting The male (shown) is blue overall; the female is uniformly dull brown. The pleasing call of this bird (*sweet-sweet, chew-chew, sweet-sweet*) is often heard from roadsides and trails at the edges of eastern forests and brushlands. (238)

Pyrrhuloxia

Rose-breasted Grosbeak

Black-headed Grosbeak

Blue Grosbeak

Indigo Bunting

59

Lazuli Bunting

Painted Bunting

Dickcissel

Evening
Grosbeak

female

male

Purple Finch

male

female

Lazuli Bunting Another blue bunting, which lives in brushy areas and along streams in the West. The male can be distinguished from the male Indigo by his white wing bars, rusty chest, and white belly. (239)

Painted Bunting A vividly colored bunting that lives in gardens and brushy areas of the southeastern U.S. The male is all red below and on the rump, with a violet head and a green back. He also has a red eye-ring. The female is entirely green. (240)

Dickcissel A sparrow-shaped bird that lives in grasslands from the Appalachians to the Rockies. As in the meadowlark, the male (shown) has a black V on his yellow breast, but has chestnut shoulders. He calls *dick dick ciss ciss ciss* from weeds in meadows and fields. (24)

Evening Grosbeak A chunky, yellowish finch with a large, ivory-colored bill. If you have a bird feeder, flocks of this bird may invade your backyard during some winters. The male has a yellow eyebrow, belly, and rump; a brownish head; and a black tail. The wings are also black with a large white wing patch. (242)

Purple Finch A raspberry-colored finch with a notched tail. The male has brown stripes on a pink back and a dark rose crown and nape. The female is all brown with white streaks and some white on her face. This finch eats buds, seeds, wild fruits, and insects in our northern woods and suburbs. (243)

House Finch A native of the West, now spreading rapidly along the Atlantic Coast. It is common in ranchlands, towns, and at bird feeders. The male has a reddish eyestripe, throat, chest, and rump, with a gray nape and back. He also has blackish stripes on his white belly. The female is streaked with brown overall, except on her head. (244)

Common Redpoll (245) (in Winter Field Scene, p. 63)

Pine Siskin A thin-billed finch with heavy brown stripes (like a sparrow). Note the white bars and yellow patches on the male's wings and at the base of his notched tail. This bird breeds in northern conifers. In winter, small flocks of siskins eat seeds of alders, birches, and cedars and visit bird feeders. (246)

American Goldfinch (247) (in Winter Field Scene, p. 63)

Lesser Goldfinch A western goldfinch with bright yellow underparts. The males are usually black above with white wing patches. In some races the male's back is green. (248)

Red Crossbill Note the long pointed bill with crossed tips, which is useful for opening cones to get the seeds inside. The male is brick red; the female is greenish. (249)

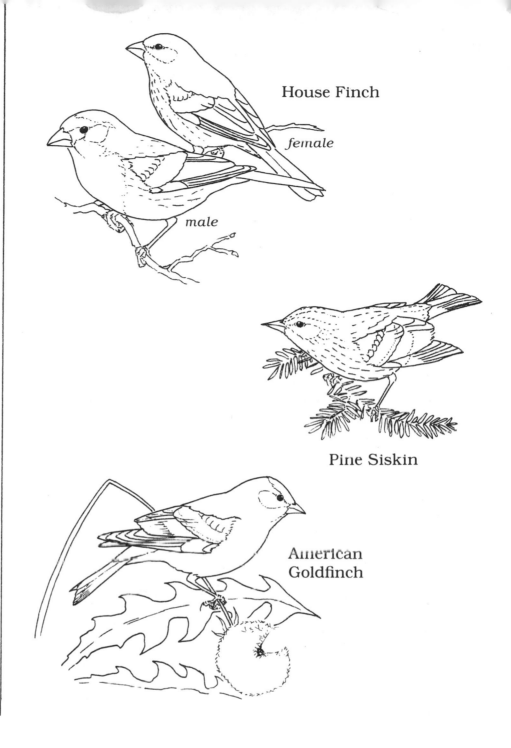

House Finch

female

male

Pine Siskin

American Goldfinch

Red Crossbill

Lesser Goldfinch

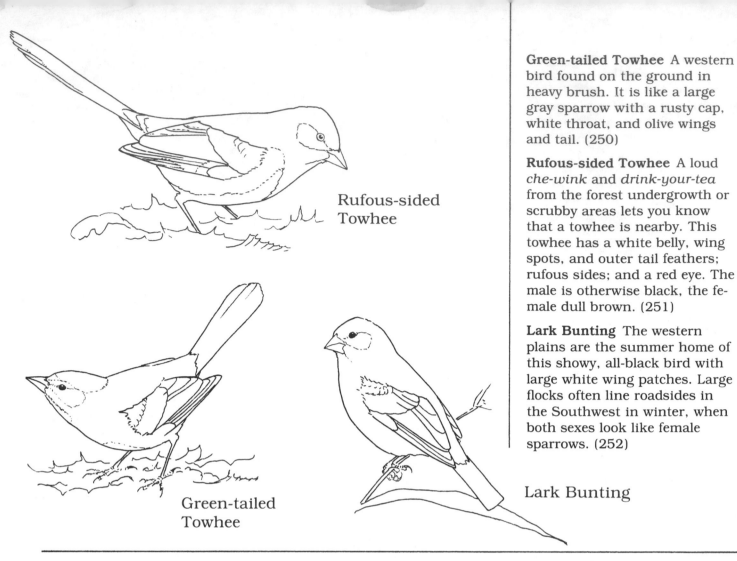

Rufous-sided
Towhee

Green-tailed
Towhee

Lark Bunting

Green-tailed Towhee A western bird found on the ground in heavy brush. It is like a large gray sparrow with a rusty cap, white throat, and olive wings and tail. (250)

Rufous-sided Towhee A loud *che-wink* and *drink-your-tea* from the forest undergrowth or scrubby areas lets you know that a towhee is nearby. This towhee has a white belly, wing spots, and outer tail feathers; rufous sides; and a red eye. The male is otherwise black, the female dull brown. (251)

Lark Bunting The western plains are the summer home of this showy, all-black bird with large white wing patches. Large flocks often line roadsides in the Southwest in winter, when both sexes look like female sparrows. (252)

Winter Field Scene

Even on cold winter days when the ground is blanketed with snow, shrubs, leftover grasses, and cornstalks protrude above the whiteness. A number of birds stay around in small flocks to feed on leftover seeds and grain. Many of them have charming, tinkling call notes that will gladden your frozen ears.

Horned Lark Flocks of larks can be seen on many of our fields, pastures, and coastal dunes. They are buff-colored birds with black, white, and yellow heads. The tiny black ear tufts (or "horns") are present only in the adults. (138)

Common Redpoll Flocks of this Arctic-breeding bird filter into weedfields of our northern states in winter. Both sexes have brown stripes on a whitish body. They also have a yellow bill, a black chin, and a red crown. The male has a rosy breast. (245)

American Goldfinch The notched black tail and white wing bars (on black wings) are distinguishing features of this tiny bird with the undulating flight. In winter (as shown in the scene on p. 63), the male is pale greenish yellow like the female. In summer he is bright yellow with a black forehead (as shown on p. 61). (247)

Snow Bunting The high Arctic tundra is the summer home of this white finch with a black back. We see flocks of these birds on our northern plains and coastal marshes in winter, when they are brownish on the crown, ears, and breast. (253)

Northern Junco A variety of differently colored subspecies of this "snowbird" live in cooler parts of North America. All have white bellies, with white outer tail feathers and dark eyes. Eastern birds are otherwise gray, with a pink bill. (254)

Chipping Sparrow A widespread small sparrow with a monotonous long trill for a call. Note the chestnut cap, the white stripe over the eye, the black line through the face, and the unstreaked gray breast and rump. (257)

American Tree Sparrow Seen by most of us only in winter, in fields and at bird feeders in the northern U.S. It looks like a large Chipping Sparrow with a black breast spot, gray eyebrow, and a bill that is black above and yellow below. (258)

245 ♂

258

247 ♂ in winter

253 ♂ in winter

138

257

254

Savannah
Sparrow

Lark Sparrow

White-crowned
Sparrow

Song Sparrow

Fox Sparrow

White-throated
Sparrow

Savannah Sparrow A small sparrow of open grasslands and weedfields. It has a yellow eye-stripe, pink legs, and a notched tail. Its call is a high, insectlike *tsit-tsit-tsit, swee-zeee*. (255)

Lark Sparrow A large sparrow that lives west of the Appalachians. It has a chestnut stripe on the head, a solid whitish breast with one black diamond, and a long black tail with white outer tail feathers. It lives around farms, orchards, and fields with scattered bushes. (256)

Chipping Sparrow (257) (in Winter Field Scene, p. 63)

American Tree Sparrow (258) (in Winter Field Scene, p. 63)

White-throated Sparrow The pleasing song of *Old Sam Peabody, Peabody, Peabody* is familiar to hikers in our northern woods and mountains. This sparrow commonly winters in the South and East, where its large size, white throat (surrounded by gray underparts), and yellow lores make it easy to recognize. (259)

White-crowned Sparrow A large sparrow with a clear, pale gray breast. The head is small, with black and white stripes and a pink bill. This sparrow is abundant in the West, somewhat rarer in the East. (260)

Song Sparrow A common sparrow in wetter scrub and fields throughout North America. It has a black spot on the breast, like the Tree and Lark Sparrows, but is heavily streaked with brown below. It repeats its pleasant song up to seven times a minute. (261)

Fox Sparrow A very large, brown-streaked sparrow that looks like a Brown Thrasher, except for its bill. It inhabits dense woodland thickets, where it kicks leaf litter, the way a towhee does. (262)

Numbers are keyed to captions throughout the book.

Numbers are keyed to captions throughout the book.